THIS PAGE IS INTENTIONALLY LEFT BLANK

TABLE OF CONTENTS

I) ABOUT THE MENTOR

Hi, I am Amer Ali. As a PMI® authorized training partner and project management expert, I have led various project management events and trained over 10,000+ resources in 5+ countries.

I offer training in several PMI certifications including PMP®, PgMP®, RMP®, SP®, PBA®, ACP®, and DASSM®. In addition to my training expertise, I have also been a prominent keynote speaker who has addressed talks at TEDx and numerous other public speaking forums.

As a mentor, I identify the candidate's strengths and build on them to establish their learning goals. I believe that anyone can become extraordinary and world-class by leveraging their strengths instead of focusing on their weaknesses. My mentorship and guidance have gained worldwide recognition for my extensive follow-up efforts. Once a candidate enrolls in one of my programs, I ensure that the students adhere to their individually customized roadmap based on their learning needs and schedule. As a result, there is no way out until the candidate becomes a successfully certified professional.

Over the past decade, I have devoted myself to facilitating people and businesses in achieving spectacular results. I have acquired a vast array of experiences that can be tailored to meet the specific needs of organizations in private, public, and social sectors across various countries and cultures.

I am always available to connect with you and provide guidance on your journey towards achieving your goals. You can find me on my socials, and I look forward to connecting with you and supporting you in your pursuit of excellence.

@ameralipmp +971588350833 ameralipmp@gmail.com

II) ABOUT THE PROJECT MANAGEMENT INSTITUTE

Project Management Institute (PMI) is the leading association for those in project, program, or portfolio management professions. They offer various resources such as guides, industry standards, articles, templates, job boards, certifications, and much more to assist professionals in their careers.

Designed by Project Managers for Project Managers, the PMP® certification is a globally recognized project management certification. It proves you have the ability to lead projects for any organization and in any industry.

The PMP® certification is a professional experience-based certification. It offers an exciting opportunity for professionals to find fulfilling and in-demand work to advance their careers and increase their earning potential with any team in any industry.

III) ABOUT OUR PROGRAM

Batch Program - US $499	1-to-1 Mentor Program US $999
▪ Instructor-Led Group Sessions ▪ Community-Based Learning ▪ Live Classroom Environment ▪ Weekend Classes ▪ Access to Premium Coaching Calls ▪ Exam Application Sign-Up Support ▪ Daily Follow Up	▪ Individual, Self-Paced Learning ▪ Access to Pre-Training Material ▪ Mentor Support 24x7 ▪ Access To Live Group Sessions ▪ Access To Premium Coaching Calls ▪ Exam Application Sign-Up Support ▪ Daily Follow Up

IV) PREFACE

The world is enhanced by the vision of those who lead and inspire others. It is, indeed, the altruistic act of sharing the gift of time to mentor future leaders that truly propels our society towards greater achievements.

As with most specialized disciplines, project management is becoming increasingly complex. It has its own jargon, approaches, professional qualifications, and communities.

Being a competent project manager requires more than just subject matter expertise. It involves the use of specific knowledge, skills, tools, and techniques to deliver something of value to people.

The need for Project management is pivotal because it ensures the right people do the right things, at the right time – it ensures proper project management process is followed throughout the project life cycle.

This book contains comprehensive mind maps that fundamentally explains the concepts of project management in an elaborative manner, helping you prepare for the PMI PMP® exam. If you are starting out on a career as a professional project manager, this book can also benefit you by demonstrating all the key knowledge that will enable you to become a successful project manager.

*This book includes a free complementary course worth $19.99 from UDEMY. Kindly drop an email to ameralipmp@gmail.com to claim your access pass!

V) ACKNOWLEDGEMENT

I would like to acknowledge the outstanding efforts of my sister, friend, and co-author, Rania Yaqub, who played a key role in the compilation of this book.

Rania was not only incredibly helpful with the detailed writing and editing, but she also worked on the creative aspects of the book and organized the information flow in a sophisticated manner. Rania adopted the book as her own and put countless hours and extraordinary efforts into its development. Her hard work, dedication, and enthusiasm have been instrumental in the success of this project.

I would like to extend my gratitude to my certified students who made this book possible. Their insightful feedback and the eagerness to add value to project management world have helped us refine our content and improve the quality of our work. I am grateful for their contributions and proud to have had the opportunity to work with such talented and committed group of individuals.

VI) OUR SUCCESS STORIES

"The pathway videos have helped me get back on track, it would have not been possible without your instructions – Durga 2023 PMP® Certified."

"I finished my training one year back but could not complete my exam due to some technical glitch and eventually lost my application date. After watching Sir Amer's videos, I contacted him, and he not only guided me through the program, but also assisted me with my exam re-application - R. Shreevatsan 2023 PMP® Certified."

"I was not a consistent learner, but your rigorous follow up forced me to become a certified professional - Saipreetha 2023 PMP® Certified."

<u>1.FUNDAMENTALS</u>

What is a Project?

A project is temporary endeavor undertaken to create unique products, services, or results. It has a specific start and a specific end date. End date must be there! If the project does not have an end date, it is not considered a project. All the projects must have an end date.

What is Project Management?

Project management is a collection of processes that includes initiating a new project, planning, putting the project management plan into action, and measuring progress and performance. Project management is an integrative undertaking that requires each project and product process to be appropriately aligned and connected with the other processes to facilitate coordination. It involves identifying the project requirements, establishing project objectives, balancing constraints, and taking the needs and expectations of the key stakeholders into consideration.

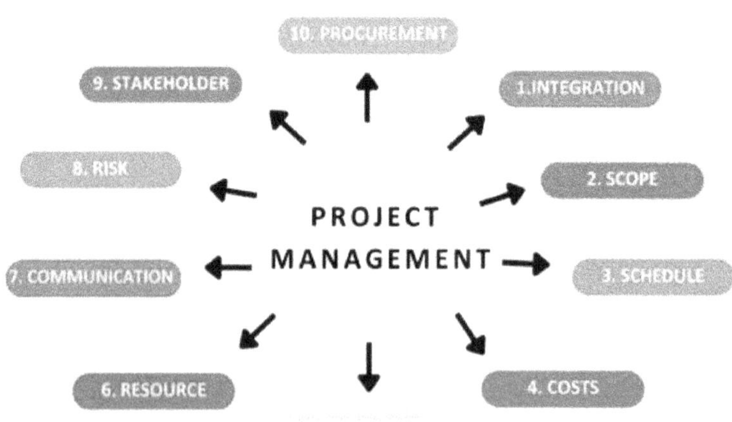

Characteristics of Project

- Projects are unique.
- Projects are temporary in nature and have a definite beginning and ending date.
- Projects are completed when the project goals are achieved, or it is determined the project is no longer viable.
- A successful project is one that meets the expectations of your stakeholders.
- Projects initiate change in the organization.
- Projects bring about business value creation.

Need For Project?

- Customer requirement.
- Legal requirement.
- Market demand.
- Organization demand

Why are Projects even started?

Projects are started to achieve some goal and to add value as well as it improves business or market value. When considering whether you have a project on your hands, you need to keep some issues in mind. First, is it a project or an ongoing operation? Next, if it is a project, who are the stakeholders? And third, what characteristics distinguish this endeavor as a project?

Project Performance Domain

The eight project performance domains form an integrated system to enable successful delivery of the project and intended outcomes.

Stakeholders A project is successful when it achieves its objectives by producing deliverables that meet the expectations of the stakeholders.	**Project Work** Establish project processes, manage physical resources, and foster a learning environment
Team The people responsible for producing project deliverables that realize business outcome	**Delivery** Delivering the scope and quality that the project was undertaken to achieve
Development Approach and Life Cycle Development approach, cadence, and life cycle phases of the project	**Measurement** Assess project performance and take appropriate actions to maintain acceptable performance
Planning Initial, ongoing, and evolving organization and coordination necessary for delivering project deliverables and outcomes	**Uncertainty** Risk and uncertainty

[Reference: A Guide to the Project Management Body of Knowledge – (PMBOK® Guide) – 7th Edition]

What are Operations?

Operations are ongoing endeavors that produce repetitive outputs, with resources assigned to do basically the same set of tasks according to the standards institutionalized in a product life cycle. Unlike the ongoing nature of operations, projects are temporary endeavors.

Project Vs. Operations

PROJECT	OPERATIONS
Temporary	Ongoing
Unique	Repetitive
Ends when objectives are met	Does not end when objectives are met

The purpose of operations is to keep the organization functioning, whereas the purpose of a project is to meet its goals and to conclude. At the completion of a project, or at various points throughout the project, the deliverables may get turned over to the organization's operational areas for ongoing care and maintenance

What is a Portfolio?

A portfolio is nothing, but a combination of projects, programs and subsidiary portfolios and operations managed as a group to achieve strategic objectives. It consists of projects, programs, sub portfolios, and operations managed as a group to achieve strategic objective.

Portfolio management encompasses centrally managing the collections of programs, projects, other work, and sometimes other portfolios. Portfolio Manager refers to the person who manages the portfolio.

What is a Program?

A program is a group of related projects subsidiary programs and program activities managed in a coordinated way to obtain benefits and control not available from managing them individually. Program management focuses on interdependencies of projects and describes the best approach to achieve program objectives. Programs are nothing but groups of related projects, subsidiary programs, and other activities that are managed using similar techniques to capitalize on benefits that would not be feasible if you managed the projects individually. The Program manager coordinates and oversees multiple interrelated projects within an organization, ensuring alignment with goals, on-time completion, and proper documentation, while managing the program team and communicating with stakeholders.

What is difference between Program and Project?

A project is typically a one-time effort that has a defined start and end date and is focused on delivering a specific output or outcome. Projects are often used to create something new, such as a product, service, or system, or to improve an existing one. A program, on the other hand, is a collection of related projects that are managed together to achieve a broader set of objectives. Programs are often used to achieve strategic goals, such as improving organizational performance, increasing efficiency, or enhancing customer satisfaction.

There are two influences that occur on the projects.

1. OPA - Organizational Process Assets
2. Organizational Structures

Organizational Process Assets (OPAs)

Plans, processes, policies, procedures, and knowledge bases specific to and used by the performing organization. These assets influence the management of the project.

- The policies of the organizations
- The procedures of the organizations
- The tools and templates
- Past lesson learned.
- The organizational database

Processes, Policies, And Procedures are:

- Established by the project management office (PMO) or another function outside of the project.
- Not updated as part of project work.
- Templates, lifecycles, and checklists can be tailored, but not updated, for a project.

Organizational Knowledge Bases are updated throughout the project with project information Updated information such as financial performance, lessons learned, performance metrics and issues, and defects.

Enterprise Environmental Factors (EEFs) are conditions (internal or external) not under the control of the project team, that influence, constrain, or direct the project at the organizational, portfolio, program, or project level.

- Mostly factors that are not within the control of the project.
- External or internal to the organization.
- Input to most planning processes.
- Can support or limit project management.

List of External and Internal EEFs:

External	Internal
• Marketplace conditions • Social and cultural influences and issues • Legal restrictions • Commercial databases • Academic research • Government or industry standards • Financial considerations • Physical environmental element	• Organizational culture, structure, and governance Geographic distribution of facilities and resources • Infrastructure • Resource availability • Employee capability

Get to Know the External Business Environment

- TECOP (Technical, Environmental, Commercial, Operational, and Political)
- VUCA (Volatility, Uncertainty, Complexity, Ambiguity).
- PESTLE (Political, Economic, Social, Technical, Legal, Environmental) it be internal and external.

These frameworks can help you to better understand external factors that can introduce risk, and uncertainty, or provide opportunities.

Internal Business Environment

Organizational changes can make a dramatic impact on the scope of a project. The project manager and project sponsor need to have visibility into business plans, reorganizations, process changes, and other internal activities as internal business changes might cause the need for new deliverables.

Project Management Information System - PMIS

A PMIS is a software program or application that organizes and controls the flow of project data and information. It is considered an internal EEF.

EEFs and OPAs

- Projects exist and operate in environments that may influence them, favorably or unfavorably.
- EEFs and OPAs are two major categories of project influences.

Organizational Influences

- Culture, style, organizational structure.
- Level of project management maturity and project management systems.
- Project-based versus non-project-based organization.
- Project manager's authority level.
- Approach for risk management activities.
- External organizations.

Organizational Structures

Just as projects are unique, so are the organizations in which they are carried out. Organizations have their own styles, cultures, and ways of communicating that influence how project work is performed and their ability to achieve project success. Because uniqueness abounds in business cultures, you are likely to find any number of organizational structures. Some of the elements that help frame an organizational structure include the following:

- Alignment with organizational objectives.
- Skills and special capabilities.
- Escalation path.
- Authority levels.

- Accountability and responsibility levels.
- Ability to adapt.
- Efficient and effective performance.
- Cost.
- Locations.
- Communications.

Project Management Office (PMO)

A PMO might exist in all organizational structures — functional, project-oriented, or matrix. It might have full authority to manage projects, including the authority to cancel projects, or it might serve only in an advisory role. PMOs might also be called project offices, program management offices, or Centers of Excellence. Types of PMOs include:

- Supportive.
- Controlling.
- Directive.

PMO Function

Supportive	Controlling	Directive
• Develop project management best practice Methodology standards and templates. • Coach, mentors, training and providing oversight to project managers.	• Monitor compliance with PM standards, policies, procedures, and templates via project audits.	• Manage shared resources. • Coordinat e communic ation across projects.

The PMO usually has responsibility for maintaining and archiving project documentation for future reference. This office compares project goals with project progress and gives feedback to the project teams and management. It ensures that projects are aligned with the strategic objectives of the organization, and it measures the performance of active projects and suggests corrective actions. The PMO evaluates completed projects for their adherence to the project management plan and asks questions like “Did the project meet the time frames established?” “Did it stay within budget?” and “Was the quality acceptable?”

Types of Organization

Organizations can be classified into two major types:

Functional: Functional organizations are centered on specialties and grouped by function, which is why they are called functional organizations. As an example, the organization might have a human resources department, finance department, marketing department, and so on. The work in these departments is specialized and requires people who have the skill sets and experience in these specialized functions to perform specific duties for the department.

Projectized: Project-oriented organizations are nearly the opposite of functional organizations. The focus of this type of organization is the project itself. The idea behind a project-oriented organization is to develop loyalty to the project, not to a functional manager.

Project managers are responsible for making decisions regarding the project and acquiring and assigning resources. The PM have complete authority to decide the following constraints in projectized organization:

- Resource
- Budget
- Priority

Relative Authority in Organizational Structures

RELATIONSHIP	FUNCTIONAL	MATRIX	PROJECT-ORIENTED
Team members report to	Functional department	Conflicted loyalty	Project
Team members report to	Functional manager	Both functional manager and project manager	Project manager
Project manager's role is	Part-time	Full-time	Full-time
Team members' role is	Part-time	Part-time	Full-time
Control of project manager over team members is	Low	Medium	High

[The table above states the Project Manager's authority relative to the functional manager's authority over the project and the project team]

Matrix Organization Variations

Matrix organizations came about to minimize the differences between, and take advantage of, the strengths and weaknesses of functional and project-oriented organizations. The idea at play here is that the best of both organizational structures can be realized by combining them into one. Essentially, there are three types:

- **Weak Matrix:** Functional managers have the majority of power in this structure, Project manager is more of a coordinator or expeditor/facilitator.

- **Strong Matrix:** PM is full-time with authority, control, and project Strong matrix administrative staff – but functional manager still involved.

- **Balanced Matrix:** The power is balanced between project managers and functional managers. Each manager has responsibility for their parts of the project or organization, and employees are assigned to projects based on the needs of the project, not the strength or weakness of the manager's position. PM is acknowledged but does not have complete control over the project or budget funds.

There are two things to consider when initiatives first begin.
1) Product
2) Project

Understanding the Project Life Cycle

A project life cycle is the series of phases that a project passes through from its initiation to its closure. A life cycle can be documented within a methodology. The project life cycle can be determined or shaped by the unique aspects of the organization, industry, or technology employed.

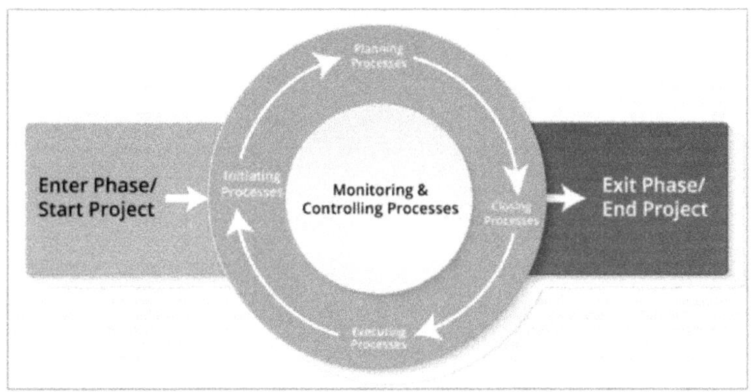

Project Phases

A project phase is a set of interrelated project activities that are grouped together to achieve a specific objective. These activities are usually carried out in a sequential manner, although there may be some overlap in certain cases. The completion of a project phase typically results in the achievement of a deliverable or milestone. Phases are usually sequential, with the prior phase being essentially complete before the start of the next phase. The number of phases in a project typically ranges from four to five, depending on the methodology employed. These phases include initiation, planning, execution, monitoring and control, and closure.

Phase Reviews/Phase Gate/Kill Point

Project phases evolve through the life cycle in a series of phase sequences called handoffs, or technical transfers. For projects that consist of sequential phases, the end of one phase typically marks the beginning of the next.

A phase review should be held at the end of each phase. This allows the project manager, stakeholders, and project sponsor the opportunity to determine whether the project should continue to the next phase. They will examine the progress performance to date against the project charter, the business case, the project management plan, and the benefits management plan. As each phase is completed, it is handed off to the next phase.

Phase Completion

You will recognize phase completion because each phase has a specific deliverable, or multiple deliverables, which marks the end of the phase. A deliverable is an output that must be produced, verified, and approved to bring the phase, life-cycle process, or project to completion. It might also include things such as design documents, project budgets, blueprints, project schedules, prototypes, and so on.

Process Group for Project Management

A project management process group is a logical grouping of project management to achieve specific objectives. They are independent of project phases. All these process groups have individual processes that collectively make up the group.

- **Initiation:** - Identifies the need for project, establishes business case.
- **Planning:** - Define project objectives, establish scope, plan how project will be executed and closed.
- **Execution:** - Perform the work.
- **Monitoring & Control:** - Track and review progress. Ensure compliance. Perform integrated change management.
- **Closing:** - Finalize all project activities, formally close phase, or project.

Business Needs Documents

- Created in advance of the project's launch and frequently evaluated.
- Information sources regarding the goals of the project and how it contributes to corporate objectives.

Business Case

A business case is a document you create that details all the benefits and expected costs. Typically, the business case examines the financial and non-financial criteria that are used to assess whether the organization will commit to the project. The business case must be correctly based on the knowledge available at the time it is created, be unbiased, and clear. The business environment and customer requirements information are necessary to build the foundation of the business case. Understanding the needs of the customer as well as the state of the environment within which the business operates is needed to position and differentiate the project outcome being proposed. This requires quality information about the following:

- The Business Environment.
- Customer Requirements.
- Business Strategy.
- Business Success Criteria.
- Provides business information to determine whether result of project is worth required investment.
- Business need and cost-benefit analysis are used to justify project and establish project boundaries.

Business Case	Business Needs Documents
• Documented economic feasibility study	• Provide high -level deliverables
• Establishes benefits of project components	• Prerequisite of formal business case
• Provides a basis for authorization of further project activities	• Describe requirements - what needs creating or performing

Benefits Management Plan

A document that describes how and when the benefits of a project will be derived and measured. Benefits management is about realizing the business results desired from the investment in a project. It is about management of the business goals that are driving the need for a project and the achievement of the business results intended.

Target Benefits	Expected tangible and intangible business value to be realized from the project
Strategic Alignment	How the benefits align with the organization's business strategies
Timeframe	When the benefits (short-term and long-term) will be realized, usually by project phase
Benefits Owner	Person or group that monitors, records, and reports the benefits
Metrics	Direct and indirect measurements of the realized benefits
Risks	Risks associated with achieving the targeted benefits

Business Value

The business value refers to the sum of all tangible and intangible values within an organization. It can include all capital assets of an organization as well as intangible elements such as brand recognition.

Value Analysis

Value analysis is the process of examining each of the components of business value and understanding cost of each one. The goal is to cost-effectively improve the components to increase the overall business value.

Cost- Benefit Analysis

A systematic approach to estimating the strengths and weaknesses of alternatives used to determine options which provide the best approach to achieving benefits while preserving savings.

- Frequently used to compare potential projects to determine which one to authorize.
- Select the alternative which demonstrates that benefits outweigh costs by the greatest amount.
- Alternative should not be chosen when costs exceed benefits.
- The accuracy of the estimates of cost and benefit determines the value of the benefit-cost analysis.

Benefit Realization

- Clearly identified goals.
- Properly planned route to reach them.
- Milestones along the way to mark progress.
- Criteria or defined targets against which to report success.
- See program management standard, benefit realization practice guide.
- Projects results usage benefit.

Benefit Measurement Methods

Business-based (choose smallest number)

- Payback period
- Opportunity cost
- Financial based (choose largest number)
- Time value of money (PV, FV, NPV)
- Internal rate of return (IRR)
- Return on Investment (ROI)

A financial metric of profitability that measures the gain or loss from an investment relative to the amount of money invested. Sometimes called the rate of return. Usually expressed as a percentage.

Net Present Value (NPV)

- NPV = salary- expense.
- NPV = Cash inflow - cash outflow.
- Net present value for our project should be positive.
- Minimum it should be zero.
- It should never be negative.

Internal Rate of Return (IRR)

- It is percentage of NPV.
- IRR = percentage cash inflow – percentage cash out.

Money

- The value of the future is called the money.
- Future value = (present value 1+ 2)^{n}
- Where n = interest rate.

The project is preceded by a business case and a benefit management strategy. These are referred to as BDs, or business documents, and come before projects. Project managers are powerless over them. The PM creates a project charter once the sponsor has given their approval.

Formal document

Formal document of the project has everything in the project at a high-level information.

- What is the scope of the project?
- Why are we doing it?

Triple Constraint

Every project has a triple restriction, which is the cost of the project, the budget, and the timeframe. Project Manager should address the competing constraints of scope, schedule, cost, resources, quality, and risk. The importance of each constraint is different for each project, and the project manager tailors the approach for managing these constraints based on the project environment, organizational culture, stakeholder needs, and other variables.

Project Management Principles

- Be diligent respectful and caring.
- Steward recognizes evaluate and respond to system interactions.
- Navigate complexity.
- Create a collaborative project team environment.
- Demonstrate leadership behaviors.
- Optimize risk responses.

- Effectively engage with stakeholders.
- Tailor based on context.
- Embrace adaptability and resiliency.
- Focus on value.
- Build equality into process and deliverables.
- Enable change to achieve the envisioned the future state.

Needs Assessment

- Precedes the business case.

  Involves understanding of:
- Business goals and objectives.
- Issues and opportunities.
- Analysis of situation as required, desired or optional.
- Recommends proposals to address.
- What should be done?
- Constraints, assumptions, risks, and dependencies.
- Success measures.
- Implementation approach.

Project Charter

A document issued by the project initiator or sponsor that formally authorizes the existence of a project and provides the project manager with the authority to apply organizational resources to project activities.

Project Charter Contents:

- Measurable project objectives and related success criteria.
- High-level requirements.
- High-level project description, boundaries, and key deliverables.
- Overall project risk summary of milestone schedules.
- Pre-approved financial resources and key stakeholders list.
- Project approval requirements.
- Project exit criteria.
- Assigned project manager and responsibility/authority level.
- Name and authority of project sponsor.

Kickoff Meeting Goals:

- Establish project context.
- Assist in team formation.
- Ensure team alignment to the overall project vision.

Activities during kickoff may include:

- Defining a vision statement.
- Defining a team charter.

Assisting the Customer/Product Owner with:

- User story writing.
- Estimation of effort.
- Prioritization planning.
- Initial product backlog.

Developing a Voting Model

Voting models are best used in a facilitated work session where all critical stakeholders can be assembled and provided the opportunity to discuss and debate the value of each of the candidate projects. To facilitate the collection of discussion outcomes and information, it is best to create a work template for use in the voting event. The figure below illustrates numerous examples of voting methods that can be used to reach a consensus.

Method	Best for	How It Works
Fist of Five	Expression of range of agreement	Closed fist = complete disagreement Fist of 5 – complete agreement
Roman Voting	Simple yes or no	Thumbs up or down (sometimes sideways for neutral)
Polling	Consider independent points of view	Hear opinions and then vote
Dot Voting	Select several options from a list	Distribute dots equally, then each person allocates dots according to highest preference

Decision Making Model

- **Unanimous Decision or Unanimity** – The term "unanimous decision" or "unanimity" is used when everyone agrees.

- **Majority** – This occurs when the majority of stakeholders agree on the decision.

- **Plurality –** This involves counting the excess of votes where the largest segment of a group decides but is not necessarily a majority. This is typically used when two or more options are being voted on.

- **Autocratic Decision –** Making involves one person making the decision on behalf of the group.

- **Multi Criteria Decision Analysis –** Is another method of making a decision where a matrix is used to analyze criteria identified ahead of time (such as risk levels valuation).

Assumptions Much of the work performed during project initiation is focused on trying to predict what will happen in the future. Assumptions in a project refer to events or circumstances that are expected to happen over the life cycle of the project but are not necessarily proven or confirmed. They are educated guesses made based on the available information and knowledge at the time of planning the project. Assumptions can be related to various aspects of a project, such as the availability of resources, the behavior of stakeholders, or the performance of technology.

Constraints are anything that either restrict the actions of the project team or dictate the actions of the project team. Everything that prevents you from moving forward is considered to be a limitation.

Functional requirements are those that describe how the product will perform. Often used in software development, it typically describes a behavior such as calculations or processes that should occur once data is entered. In non-software terms, functional requirements might describe specifications, quantities, colors, and more.

Nonfunctional requirements describe the characteristics needed for the requirement to function, such as security needs, performance, and reliability. Technically, it refers to elements that are related to the product but does not describe the product directly. In the case of a software product, this could be a security requirement or performance criteria.

Acceptance Criteria consists of the process and criteria that will be used to determine whether the deliverables and the final product, service, or results of the project are acceptable and satisfactory.

Project Deliverables refers to measurable outcomes, measurable results, or specific items that must be produced or performed to consider the project or project phase completed. Deliverables should be specific and verifiable.

SIX LEADERSHIP STYLES

In project management, the concept of servant leadership is often recommended by the Project Management Institute (PMI), as it emphasizes the importance of prioritizing the needs of team members and creating a positive work environment. However, it is important to consider each of the other leadership styles individually and their potential impact on the project.

1. LAISSEEZ-FAIRE - Time Decisions Hands Off Approach

- Leaders provide little or no direction or no supervision.
- Teams are given with as much as much.
- Freedom as possible team makes decision and resolves problems on their own.
- The leaders appear absent when it comes to project decisions.

2. **TRANSACTIONAL** - managerial leadership rewards and punishments

3. **SERVANT LEADER - Carry Food and Water**

- Focusing on putting team first.
- Providing growth opportunity.
- This method inspires employees.
- Enrich lives of individuals and build better organizations.

4. **TRANSFORMATIONAL - Inspiring and Encourage Innovation**

- Leader works with subordinates to identify needed change.
- Creates a vision to guide the chain through our inspiration and motivation.
- Execute the change with committed numbers.
- Empowerment Innovation and creativity are encouraged.

5. **CHARISMATIC LEADER - Lead by Example**

- Inspire and have high energy levels.
- Enthusiastic self-confident.
- Strong convictions about what team can achieve what team can achieve.

6. **INTERACTIONAL- Combination**

- Excited and inspired about the project work.
- Coach team and want team to be action orientated.
- Hold team accountable for results.

Project Artifacts

Project artifacts are tangible items created during a project, such as documents and materials. They serve as evidence of the work done and provide a record of the project's progress. Examples include project plans, schedules, budgets, and meeting minutes.

Project Management Methodologies

Project management is an ever-evolving field that requires a number of approaches to be successful, since no two projects are identical. There are several types of project methodologies in the project management, such as:

1. Predictive
2. Agile
3. Iterative
4. Incremental
5. Hybrid

These life cycles are created based on project scope, often referred to as demand. The following questions can help us identify what approach to implement while choosing a framework.

- Is the scope constant or changeable?
- Is the delivery all at once or in increments?
- What kind of delivery does the project need?

PRACTICE EXAM QUESTIONS

Question 1

What is the difference project and operation?

A. Project is permanent while operation is temporary.
B. Operation is permanent while Project is temporary.
C. Both are permanent.
D. Both are temporary.

Correct answer

B – Operation is permanent while Project is temporary

Question 2

Who define business value?

A. Project manager
B. Team
C. Customer
D. All of them

Correct Answer

C – Customer

Question 3

You are working in the organization and your project is within triple constraint, you are doing everything by yourself. However, when the project is completed, it is considered as failure what project manager missed in this project?

A. He missed identifying risk.
B. He did not meet quality.
C. Your stakeholders are not satisfied with the result.
D. All of them

Correct answer

C – Your stakeholders are not satisfied with the result

Question 4

Your organization has gone through massive merger as a result, new organization has formed. According to strategy of new organization, your project is not useful, sponsored shared this information what will you do?

A. Look for another job.
B. Keep doing your work.
C. Start closing the project.
D. Nothing

Correct answer

C – Start closing the project

Question 5

You are the project manager of an organization you have worked all your life in USA, you went to Middle East and found out that you cannot use WhatsApp as communication tools. What will you update?

A. PMIS
B. OPAs- Organizational Process Assets
C. Stakeholder Register
D. EEF

Correct Answer

B – OPAs

Question 6

You are the project manager of an organization; you want to start the project where will you look first?

A. PMIS
B. OPA's- organizational process assets
C. Stakeholder register
D. EEF

Correct answer

A – PMIS

Question 7

Who can make decisions regarding resource in Weak Matrix?

A. PM
B. Sponsor
C. Function manager
D. Both PM and Sponsor

Correct answer

C – Function manager

Question 8

You are working in the project, you are getting daily orders from your PMO to execute day 2-day task, which type of PMO you are working in?

A. Supportive
B. Controlling
C. Directive
D. Functional

Correct answer

C – Directive

Question 9

You are working in organization although your title is project manager, but you do not have any power and your actions sometimes as a project expeditor or project coordination. Which type of organization you are working in?

A. Functional
B. Weak matrix
C. Strong matrix
D. Projectized
E. Balanced matrix

Correct answer

B – Weak matrix

Question 10

You are working on the project, you give your team 2 hours to complete the report, next time you give them 4 hours and they are barely able to complete the same report in that time, what it is called?

A. Parkinson law
B. Behavior driven development.
C. Student syndrome
D. Fishbowl

Correct answer

A – Parkinson law

Question 11

Which document officially start the project?

A. Project charter
B. Business case
C. Benefit management plan
D. Project management plan

Correct answer

A – Project Charter

Question 12

At the end of the project, which document you will use to see whether required benefits have been attained or not?

A. Project charter.
B. Benefit management plan.
C. Project management plan.
D. Business case.

Correct answer

B – Benefit management plan

Question 13

You are working in the Project, your sponsor has called you saying that cost of the project is more than benefit, what will you do?

A. Thank him for his update and continue working.
B. Nothing.
C. Start closing the project.
D. Convince him it is not his fault, and we must keep working the project.

Correct answer

Start closing the project.

Question 14

You are working in the project, and two members have conflict about deliverables being produced. In which process groups deliverables are produced?

A. Initiation
B. Planning
C. Execution
D. Monitoring and control
E. Closing

Correct answer

C – Execution

Question 15

You are the project manager of an organization, you are facilitating team, helping them to learn new things and if there is any roadblock in the way of team working, you are trying to remove them. You let the team take most of the decision, but you do guide them how to take it, which type of leadership style are you using?

A. Transactional
B. Servant leader
C. Transformational
D. Charismatic

Correct answer

B – Servant leader

2. STAKEHOLDERS

Stakeholder Management

A stakeholder is an individual, group, or organization who may affect, be affected by, or perceive itself to be affected by a decision, activity, or outcome of a project. Stakeholders may be actively involved in the project or have interests that may be positively or negatively affected by the performance or completion of the project.

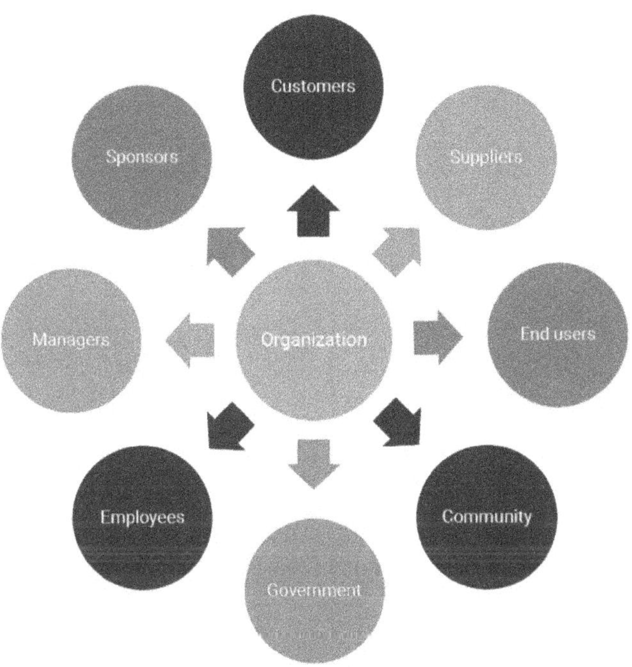

Stakeholders include all members of the project team as well as all interested entities that are internal or external to the organization. The project team identifies internal and external, positive, and negative, and performing and advising stakeholders to determine the project requirements and the expectations of all individuals involved. The project manager should manage the influences of these various stakeholders in relation to the project requirements to ensure a successful outcome.

Stakeholder Management identifies how the project will affect stakeholders, which then allows the project manager to develop several ways to effectively engage stakeholders in the project, to manage their expectations, and to ultimately achieving the project objectives. Stakeholder management is more than improving communications and requires more than managing a team. Stakeholder management is about creation and maintenance of relationships between the project team and stakeholders, with the aim to satisfy their respective needs and requirements within project boundaries.

Stakeholder Performance Domain

The stakeholder performance domain deals with stakeholder-related tasks and activities. The following expected outcomes are the result of this Performance Domain being executed effectively.

- Throughout the project, a successful working relationship with stakeholders.
- Stakeholders buy-in to the project's goal.
- Stakeholders who benefit from the project are satisfied and supportive of the stakeholder who may oppose it or its deliverables, and this does not have a detrimental impact on the project's outcomes.

How Do We Identify a Stakeholder?

To identify stakeholders, you can use various techniques and tools such as brainstorming, stakeholder maps, surveys, and interviews. Focus groups are also a useful tool for learning data collection strategies including information gathering and stakeholder mapping.

To obtain the information necessary to identify stakeholders, we need to examine each document. The secret to successful project management is finding maximum number of stakeholders on the project. If you overlook a stakeholder, it is highly likely that the project could suffer consequences. Therefore, the most important part of a project manager's job is to being aware of each stakeholder and their expectations.

Stakeholder Identification Tools and Techniques:

- External environmental factors
- Interview
- Subject Matter or Expert Asking Judgment
- Project Charter
- Organizational Process Assets
- Brainstorming

Stakeholder Register

All the identified stakeholders are recorded in the stakeholder register document. Stakeholder register could be comprehensive and formal **or** informal.

It consists of, but is not limited to the following components,

- Name
- Position
- Role
- Contact information.
- Requirement
- Expectations
- Influence
- Classification

Classification of Stakeholder

- **Upward Stakeholder**

Upward stakeholders are the stakeholders to whom you would report.

- **Downward Stakeholder**

That does not imply that you are putting someone down. No, it simply implies that they are reporting to you. Your downward stakeholder is your merchant or seller. Your vendor is regarded as a stakeholder at a lower level. You do not inform your seller about anything. The seller receives payment from you, and as a result, the seller receives payment. The vendor is working on your behalf, he is reporting to you; he is disclosing his data for you to be the vendor. Seller is an example of downward stakeholder since he is providing you with information.

- **Sideward Stakeholder**

Those who are sideways are on the same plane. Additional grouping of stakeholders can be used to rank/categorize the stakeholders such as,

- Internal stakeholders
- External stakeholder
- Within the organization
- Outside the organization
- Within the project
- Outside the project

Stakeholder Engagement

Stakeholder engagement includes implementing strategies and actions to promote productive involvement of stakeholders. Stakeholder engagement activities start before or when the project starts and continues throughout the project.

A **Stakeholder Engagement Plan** identifies the strategies and actions required to promote productive involvement of stakeholders in project or program decision making and execution.

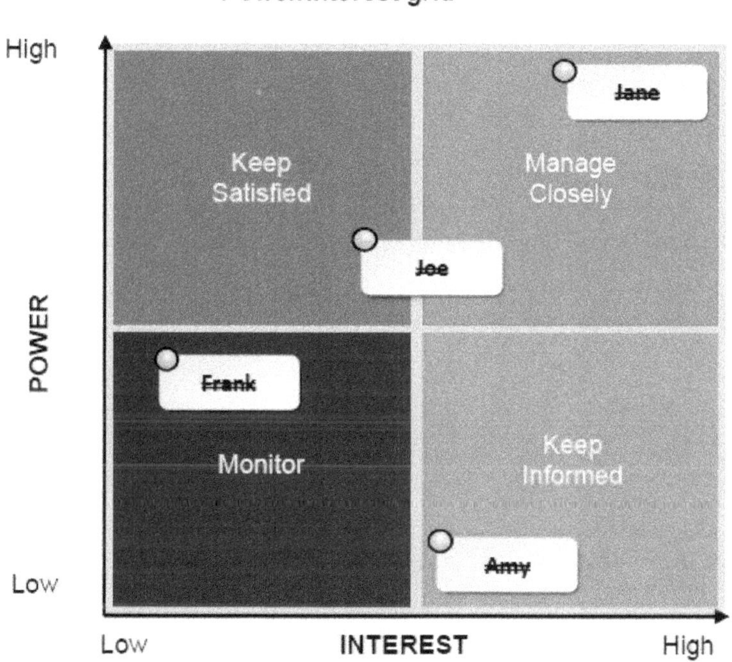

Power Interest or Power Influence Grid

Grid power interest is another name for power interest, which has the same meaning as power influence. There are four types of grid power interest.

People Having Higher Power and High Interest (Strategy: Manage Closely)

- Sponsor
- Team members
- Upward stakeholders
- Downward stakeholder

People Having High Power but Low Interested (Strategy: Keep Them Satisfied)

- Government agency
- They are interested in your project outcomes, keep them satisfied by giving them secondary information. Media is a classic example.

People Having Low Power but High Interest (Strategy: Keep Informed)

- Competitor

People Having Low Power and Low Interest (Strategy: Monitor)

- Kitchen staff
- Security guard

1- Stakeholder Cube

A stakeholder cube is fundamentally a matrix of power x interests. Any of those items that can be added are in three dimensions. Regardless of the parameter, we can gauge a person's power, interest, and attitude based on their location or by their willingness to invest in a project. We can include additional criteria such as attitude, region, language, gender, etc.

2- Salience Model

Salience model classifies stakeholders based on their level of authority, their immediate needs, and how appropriate their involvement is in terms of the project. It serves as a paradigm of power, urgency, and legitimacy. Like a stakeholder cube, it is three dimensional.

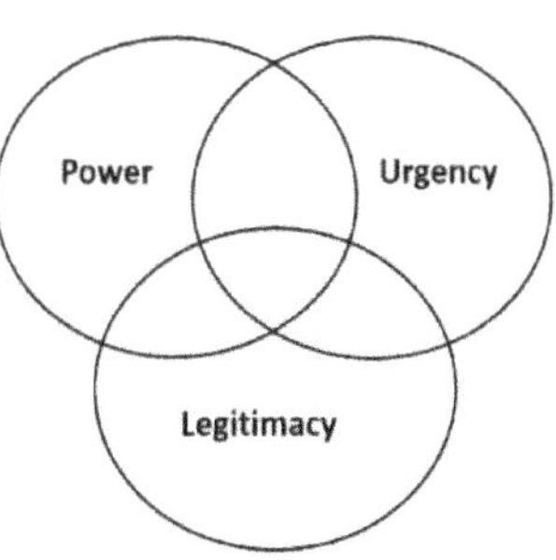

Purpose Of a Stakeholder Engagement Plan

- To manage the expectations and requirement of the stakeholder
- To engage stakeholders

We would consider stakeholders' needs and expectations when talking about them. The stakeholder could benefit from this specific project. We work to comprehend the stakeholder's preferred language. What is the most efficient strategy to interact with the stakeholder in a favorable way? The stakeholder engagement plan encompasses everything. We need to know what kind of language and format they require to accomplish that (the communication plan addresses that) but first we create a stakeholder engagement matrix. Remember, we do not disclose the stakeholder register and stakeholder engagement plan with anybody as it is highly sophisticated data of the project.

The project manager must be aware of this because certain information may be interpreted negatively by other stakeholders. The stakeholder engagement plan is therefore kept confidential.

Stakeholder Engagement Matrix

A matrix that compares current and desired stakeholder engagement levels. Stakeholder engagement matrix identifies the involvement of stakeholders at a given point in project.

- **Unaware** – unaware of project and potential impacts.
- **Resistant** – aware of project and potential impacts and resistant to change.
- **Neutral** – aware of project, but neither supportive nor resistant.
- **Supportive** – aware of project and potential impacts and supportive of work.
- **Leading** – aware of project and potential impacts and actively engaged in ensuring the project's success.

Stakeholder	Unaware	Resistant	Neutral	Supportive	Leading
Stakeholder 1	C			D	
Stakeholder 2			C	D	
Stakeholder 3				C	D

PRACTICE EXAM QUESTIONS

Question 1

You are near closing of project when sponsored emailed you that a new key stakeholder has entered the organization and he will be reviewing the success of project what you would do first.

A. Update stakeholder register
B. Update stakeholder plan
C. Update communicating plan.
D. Add this to issue log.

Correct answer

A – Update stakeholder register

Question 2

You are a project manager leading your team through a process of evaluating and classifying the current engagement levels of each stakeholder. You have a identified a stakeholder who is aware of the project but is unsupportive of the work or outcomes of the project. Within which engagement category should you advise your team to classify this stakeholder?

A. Unaware
B. Supportive
C. Resistant
D. Neutral

Correct Answer

C – Resistant

Question 3

Which of the following documents serves as the primary starting point for the development of communication requirements?

A. Communication management plan
B. Stakeholder register
C. Resource management plan

Correct Answer

B – Stakeholder register

Question 4

You want to analyze stakeholder by geography. Which tool can be useful?

A. Power influence matrix
B. Salience model
C. Stakeholder cube

Correct Answer

C – Stakeholder cube

Question 5

Which of the following is not a tool used to manage the stakeholder engagement?

A. Communication methods
B. Interpersonal skills
C. Management skills
D. Issue log

Correct Answer

D – Issue log

3. COMMUNICATIONS

Communications Management

Communication has been identified as one of the single biggest reasons for project success or failure. Effective communication within the project team and between the project manager, team members, and all external stakeholders is essential. Openness in communication is a gateway to teamwork and high performance. It improves relationships among project team members and creates mutual trust.

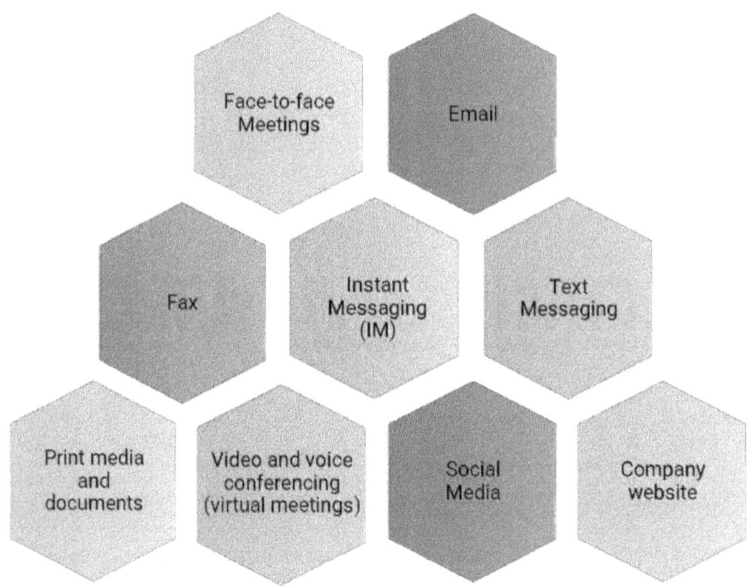

Project Communications Management includes the processes that are required to ensure timely and appropriate planning, collection, creation, distribution, storage, retrieval, management, control, monitoring, and the ultimate disposition of project information. Project managers spend most of their time communicating with team members and other project stakeholders, whether they are internal (at all organizational levels) or external to the organization.

To communicate effectively, the project manager should be aware of the communication styles of other parties, cultural nuances/norms, relationships, personalities, and the overall context of the situation. Awareness of these factors leads to mutual understanding and thus to effective communication.

Project managers should identify various communication channels, understand what information they need to provide, what information they need to receive, and which interpersonal skills will help them communicate effectively with various project stakeholders. Carrying out team-building activities to determine team member communications styles (e.g., directive, collaborative, logical, explorer, etc.), allows managers to plan their communications with appropriate sensitivity to relationships and cultural differences.

Listening is an important part of communication. Listening techniques, both active and passive give the user insight to problem areas, negotiation and conflict management strategies, decision making, and problem resolution.

Effective communication is the key to successful teams. Include communication expectations and details in the team charter. Use retrospectives to learn ways of improving communication, collaboration, and use of visibility tools.

Communication Model

The communication model used to facilitate communications and the exchange of information may vary from project to project and within various stages of the same project. A basic communication model consists of two parties, defined as the sender and receiver. Medium is the technology medium and includes the mode of communication while noise includes any interference or barriers that might compromise the delivery of the message. The sequence of steps in a basic communication model is,

- **Encode.** Thoughts or ideas are translated (encoded) into language by the sender.

- **Transmit Message.** This information is then sent by the sender using communication channel (medium).The transmission of this message may be compromised by numerous factors (e.g., distance, unfamiliar technology, inadequate infrastructure, cultural difference, and lack of background information). These factors are collectively termed as noise.

- **Decode.** The message is translated by the receiver back into meaningful thoughts or ideas.

- **Acknowledge.** Upon receipt of a message, the receiver may signal (acknowledge) receipt of the message, but this does not necessarily mean agreement with or comprehension of the message.

- **Feedback/Response.** When the received message has been decoded and understood, the receiver encodes thoughts and ideas into a message and then transmits this message to the original sender.

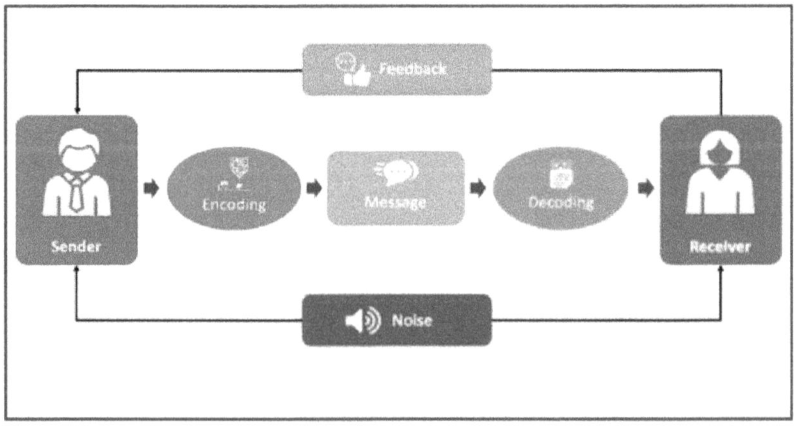

[Reference: SketchBubble Presentations]

Types of Communication

There are several communication methods that are used to share information among project stakeholders. Based on the stakeholders' communication requirements, the project manager decides how, when, and which of these communication methods are to be used in the project. Some of the methods are broadly classified as follows:

- **Push Communication**

Sent to specific recipients who need to receive the information. This ensures that the information is distributed but does not ensure that it reached or was understood by the intended audience. Push communications include letters, memos, reports, emails, faxes, voice mails, blogs, press releases, etc.

- **Pull Communication**

Used for exceptionally large volumes of information, or for exceptionally large audiences, and requires the recipients to access the communication content at their own discretion. These methods include intranet sites, e-learning, lessons learned databases, knowledge repositories, etc.

- **Interactive Communication**

Between two or more parties performing a multidirectional exchange of information. It is the most efficient way to ensure a common understanding by all participants on specified topics, and includes meetings, phone calls, instant messaging, video conferencing, etc.

The choices of communication methods that are used for a project may need to be discussed and agreed upon by the project stakeholders based on communication requirements; cost and time constraints; and familiarity and availability of the required tools and resources that may be applicable to the communications process. Communication plays a crucial role in their employment because it requires them to comprehend, work in diverse areas, and communicate in those different environments. As a result, their job becomes significant.

Communication Classification

- Team
- Stakeholder

Communication Requirement

The analysis of the communication requirements determines the information needs of the project stakeholders. These requirements are defined by combining the type and format of information needed with an analysis of the value of that information. Project resources should be expended only on communicating information that contributes to the success of the project or where a lack of communication can lead to failure. It is especially important to recognize which type of communication a stakeholder requires.

- Formal communication
- Informal communication- According to PMI, email is an informal communication.
- Written Communication
- Verbal Communication, also known as oral.
- Video Communication

Need for Communication

Planning the project communications is important to the ultimate success of any project. Inadequate communications planning may lead to problems such as delay in message delivery, communication of information to the wrong audience, or insufficient communication to the stakeholders and misunderstanding or misinterpretation of the message communicated.

On most projects, communication planning is performed early, such as during project management plan development. This allows appropriate resources, such as time and budget, to be allocated to communication activities. Effective communication means that the information is provided in the right format, at the right time, to the right audience, and with the right impact. Efficient communication means providing only the information that is needed. The seven Cs of communication is a list of principles for written and spoken communications to ensure that the communication is effective.

While all projects share the need to communicate project information, the information needs and methods of distribution may vary widely. In addition, the methods of storage, retrieval, and ultimate disposition of the project information need to be considered and appropriately documented during this process. Important considerations that may need to be taken into account include, but are not limited to:

- Who needs what information, and who is authorized to access that information.
- When they will need the information.
- Where the information should be stored.
- What format the information should be stored in.
- How the information can be retrieved.

- Geography - whether time zone, language barriers, and cross-cultural considerations need to be taken into account.
- Diversity - dealing with people from different countries is diversity. It can take the form of race, gender, or religious differences.
- Culture - when communicating, one should adhere to cultural standards. Culture is the beliefs and behaviors of one group.

As part of the communications process, the sender is responsible for the transmission of the message, ensuring the information being communicated is clear and complete, and confirming the communication is correctly understood. The receiver is responsible for ensuring that the information is received in its entirety, understood correctly, and acknowledged or responded to appropriately.

Communication Tool

There are several considerations that determines which communication tool to use.

- **Urgency of the need for information.** There is a need to consider the urgency, frequency, and format of the information to be communicated as they may vary from project to project and within various stages of a project.
- **Availability of technology.** There is a need to ensure that the technology that is required to facilitate communication is compatible, available, and accessible for all stakeholders throughout the life of the project.
- **Ease of Use.** There is a need to ensure that the choice of communication technologies is suitable for project participants and that appropriate training events are planned for, where appropriate.
- **Project environment.** There is a need to determine if the team will meet and operate on a face-to-face basis or in a virtual environment; whether they will be located in one or multiple

time zones; whether they will use multiple languages for communication; and finally, whether there are any other project environmental factors, such as culture, which may affect communications.

- **Sensitivity and confidentiality of the information.** There is a need to determine if the information to be communicated is sensitive or confidential and whether additional security measures need to be taken. Also, the most appropriate way to communicate the information should be considered.

Communications Management Plan

The communications management plan provides guidance and information on managing stakeholder expectations. A good Communication management plan entails the four R,

- Right information
- Right time
- Right impact
- Right people

The most crucial part of a communication management strategy is that it will also tell you who has the authority to share information and how it will be shared and saved as well as where and when it will be shared and stored. Your planning step is complete once you have created the communication management plan.

Implementation Of Communications Management Plan

Who is the communication authority? Information is sent to everyone in accordance with the communication management plan. Project management office is referred to as manage communications. Manage communication is used to bring and disseminate all information.

The information that is disseminated in the project moves through controlled communication and is described in the communication management plan. Since how information will be discarded in sensitive projects, government projects, and confidential projects is an important and crucial point, it must be written in a plan and implemented in the communication management when you implement them now. Communication management plans should therefore describe how this information is being delivered, when it will be received, stored, retrieved, where it will be stored, and how that information will be discarded.

Components of Communications Management Plan

- Stakeholder communications requirements
- Information to be communicated, including language to be used.
- Time frame and frequency
- Reason for distribution of information
- Person or groups who will receive information.
- Methods or technologies of conveyance
- Time and budget allocation
- Escalation process for issues that need visibility.
- Update procedure for the plan
- Glossary of common terminology
- Flowcharts depicting flow of information.
- Constraints due to regulation or policies

Monitor the Communication Plan

The project manager monitors and controls communications throughout the entire project life cycle to ensure the information needs of the project stakeholders are met. The key benefit of this process is that it ensures an optimal information flow among all communication participants, at any moment in time. Variance in communication can occur because of the following reason,

- Deviation from original plan.
- The original plan is not effective.

The plan can be altered for the following reasons, but not limited to:

- Take preventative measures.
- Plan correction through corrective action.

Work Performance Data refers to the raw observations and measurements identified during activities being performed to carry out the project work. It concludes the data on work performance as raw information since it is recorded without any editing**.** Therefore, it organizes and summarizes the information gathered, and presents the results of comparative analysis to the performance measurement baseline.

Work Performance Information organizes and summarizes the performance data gathered. This performance data typically provides status and progress information on the project at the level of detail required by the various stakeholders. This information is then communicated to the appropriate stakeholders.

Work Performance Report takes information from performance measurements and analyze it to provide project work performance information including variance analysis, earned value data, and forecasting data intended to generate decisions, raise issues, actions, or awareness. This data points could be impactful in controlling performance related risks. Information is created by converting data into a report, which is sent through control communication.

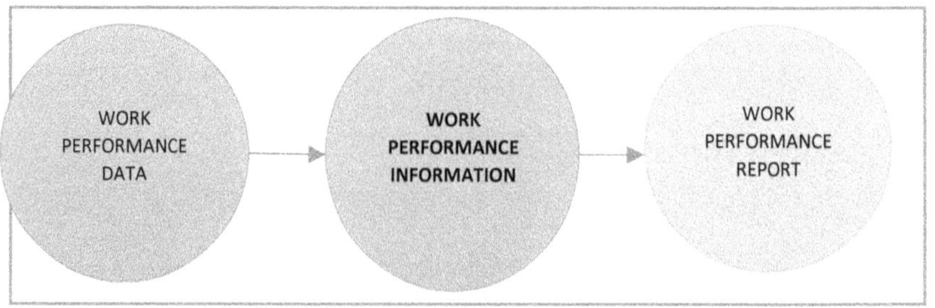

Communication Channel

The project manager should consider the number of potential communication channels or paths as an indicator of the complexity of a project's communications.

The total number of potential communication channels is n(n-1)/2, where *n* represents the number of stakeholders. It is calculated by formula,

Communication channel = n(n-1)/2

Comparison between Stakeholder and Communication Plan.

Stakeholder	Communication Plan
Stakeholder engagement level and matrix	Frequency
Current and desired engagement	Format
Strategies required to satisfy stakeholder	Language
Updated as first thing when new stakeholder is identified.	Diversity

PRACTICE EXAM QUESTIONS

Question 1

You are in a meeting with 8 key stakeholders and 2 team members, how many communications channel are there.

A. Cannot be calculated from this information.
B. 55
C. 45
D. 25

Correct answer

A – 55 is the correct answer.

Question 2

What is the best way of communication?

A. Video conference
B. Email
C. Calling to each other
D. Recording a video and

Correct answer

A – Video conference

Question 3

A new key stakeholder has been identified and stakeholder register has been updated it, what is the next logical step.

A. Raise a change request.
B. Update communication plan
C. Update stakeholder engagement plan
D. Update stakeholder register

Correct answer

A – Raise a change request.

Question 4

A new important stakeholder has been identified, you have update register, you are in planning stage, what will you do next.

A. Raise a change request.
B. Update communication plan
C. Update stakeholder engagement plan
D. Update stakeholder register

Correct Answer

C – Update stakeholder engagement plan

Question 5

A stakeholder is upset and have complained it to sponsor that is receiving every little information about the project, what the project manager should do.

A- Update communication management plan
B- Update stakeholder engagement plan
C- Update stakeholder register
D- Update lesson learned register.

Correct Answer

A – Update communication management plan

4.TEAMS

Teams Management

Project managers play a crucial role in identifying, building, maintaining, motivating, leading, and inspiring project teams to achieve high performance and meet project objectives. Effective teamwork is essential for project success, and it is the project manager's primary responsibility to develop effective project teams. To facilitate teamwork, project managers should create an environment that encourages collaboration and cooperation. They should motivate their team by providing challenges, opportunities, timely feedback, and support as needed, and by recognizing and rewarding good performance.

In today's global environment, project managers work on projects characterized by cultural diversity, with team members who may have diverse industry experience and speak multiple languages. The project management team should leverage cultural differences, focus on developing and sustaining the project team throughout the project life cycle, and promote interdependent collaboration in an atmosphere of mutual trust. Developing the project team enhances people skills, technical competencies, and overall team performance, and requires clear, timely, effective, and efficient communication between team members throughout the project's life.

Developing Project Team

Acquiring and developing the right project team is all above improving competencies, team member interaction, and overall team environment to enhance project performance. The key benefit of this process is that it results in improved teamwork, enhanced people skills and competencies, motivated employees, reduced staff turnover rates, and improved overall project performance.

The human resource management plan provides guidance on how project human resources should be defined, staffed, managed, controlled, and eventually released. It identifies training strategies and plans for developing the project team. Items such as rewards, feedback, additional training, and disciplinary actions can be added to the plan because of ongoing team performance assessments and other forms of project team management.

It is important to acknowledge that team members possess varying levels of talent. Therefore, it is necessary to evaluate their skills and determine which team members are required for the project. The number of team members needed is determined by the number of skills required. The resource calendar plays a crucial role in identifying the types of team members needed, the necessary skills, and whether physical or virtual team members are required. Additionally, resource calendars help identify times when project team members can participate in team development activities.

Virtual Teams

The use of virtual teams creates new possibilities when acquiring project team members. Virtual teams can be defined as groups of people with a shared goal who fulfill their roles with little or no time spent meeting face to face. The availability of communication technology such as e-mail, audio/video conferencing, social media, and web-based meetings has made virtual teams feasible. The virtual team model makes it possible to:

- Form teams of people from the same organization who live in widespread geographic areas.

• Add special expertise to a project team even though the expert is not in the same geographic area.

• Incorporate employees who work from home offices.

• Form teams of people who work different shifts, hours, or days.

• Include people with mobility limitations or disabilities; and

• Move forward with projects that would have been ignored due to travel expenses.

There are some disadvantages related to virtual teams, such as possibility for misunderstandings, feeling of isolation, difficulties in sharing knowledge and experience between team members, and cost of appropriate technology. Communication planning becomes increasingly important in a virtual team environment. Additional time may be needed to set clear expectations, facilitate communications, develop protocols for resolving conflict, include people in decision making, understand cultural differences, and share credit in successes. We can select a physical, virtual, or hybrid option.

Difference between Virtual Team vs. Physical Team?

- Physical team is based together, the virtual team is not.
- Virtual—with whom we cannot communicate in the same place.
- The virtual team looks at a separate area.
- Remote team members from different geographic locations interact in person.
- Virtual team members are team members who are dispersed across the globe and work from various locations.

What Are the Challenges of Virtual Team?

- Background noise
- Internet or connectivity issues
- Body language
- Different time zone
- Culture
- Multitasking
- Communication path
- Communication issues
- Team issues
- Time
- Languages
- Coordination
- Communication style

What Are the Challenges of Physical Team?

- Residence
- Food
- Physical conflicts
- Cultural issues
- Religious issues
- Recreational activities
- Geopolitical situations

There are different challenges for virtual and physical team depending upon the requirement. Requirements depend upon the,

- Budget
- Project

Team Building

As an ongoing process, team building is crucial to project success. While team building is essential during the initial stages of a project, it is a never-ending process. Changes in a project environment are inevitable, and to manage them effectively, a continued or a renewed team-building effort should be applied. The project manager should continually monitor team functionality and performance to determine if any actions are needed to prevent or correct various team problems.

Tuckman ladder

One of the models used to describe team development is the Tuckman ladder (Tuckman, 1965; Tuckman & Jensen, 1977), which includes five stages of development that teams may go through. Although it is common for these stages to occur in order, it is not uncommon for a team to get stuck in a particular stage or slip to an earlier stage. Projects with team members who worked together in the past may skip a stage.

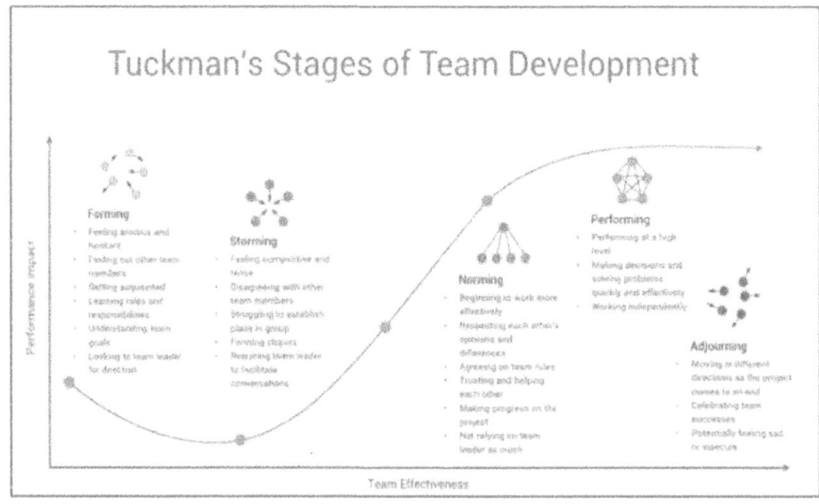

[Reference: Nulivo Presentations; Tuckman Team Development Model]

GROUND RULES

This phase is where the team meets and learns about the project and their formal roles and responsibilities. Team members tend to be independent and not as open in this phase.

- Norms and behaviours
- Respect diversity
- Respect time zones
- It is unacceptable to allow abuse when certain team members are speaking.
- The other team members remain silent when certain team members are speaking.

There are several types of ground rules depending on whether the teams are physical or virtual. There are many different kinds of ground rules that are developed, initially by the project manager. The group begins establishing ground rules for them, by which they must abide.

Team charter

A document known as a team charter, working agreement, or ground rule is one that has been written about. The team charter's section on ground rules is true. As soon as we establish the team's ground rules and charter, we make sure that every team member agrees with it.

Training Needs Assessment

Training includes all activities designed to enhance the competencies of the project team members. Training can be formal or informal. Examples of training methods include classroom, online, computer-based, on-the-job training from another project team member, mentoring, and coaching.

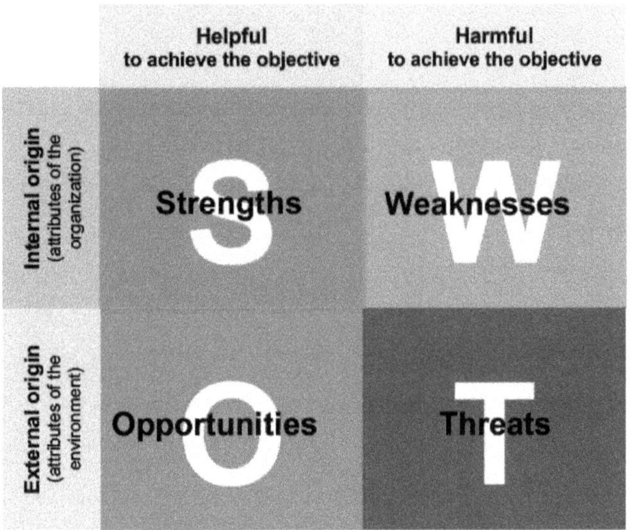

If project team members lack the necessary management or technical skills, such skills can be developed as part of the project work. Scheduled training takes place as stated in the human resource management plan. Unplanned training takes place because of observation, conversation, and project performance appraisals conducted during the controlling process of managing the project team.
Training costs could be included in the project budget, or supported by performing organization if the added skills may be useful for future projects. It could be performed by in-house or external trainers.

While the team is present, the project manager performs needs assessment throughout. He recognizes,

- What are the team members' training requirements?
- What kind of initial training are the team members most in need of?

We focus on the team's overall training during the forming phase, and as the project progresses, we work on the individual training.

Team Training includes,

- Building activities
- Diversity training
- Health and safety induction
- Ground rules training
- Cultural trainings
- Emotional Intelligence

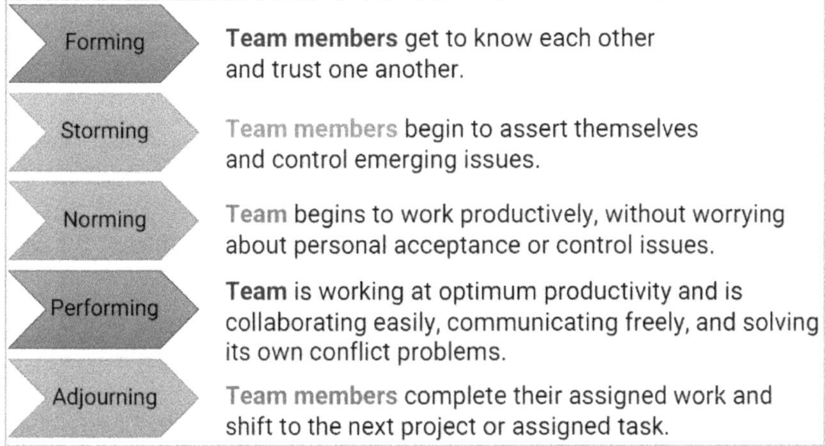

Once the training requirements of the team members have been determined, training is arranged for the entire team to meet their skill requirements. Instead of individual training, we train the entire team when it is being formed. We begin by providing training to every team member while we are in the process. Since the project manager is really leading the entire team, his function is more directive in character. This is the forming stage.

In the Forming stage, every team member makes an effort to contribute their best. They are not a cohesive squad. They are carrying out the tasks on their own. Nonetheless, each team member is giving their best effort on a personal level. Striving to provide the maximum they can. Hence, productivity exists.

However, we need to set ground rules for ourselves as individuals who are still forming. At this stage, a team charter is created.

2. Storming Stage

During this phase, the team begins to address the project work, technical decisions, and the project management approach. If team members are not collaborative and open to differing ideas and perspectives, the environment can become counterproductive. This is the longest or most crucial portion of the team because numerous abilities are needed here. Being an attentive listener is the first thing you must do in this situation if you want to manage a project.

What is Active Listening?

Active listening entails paying attention to the feelings of the individuals being spoken to as well as their words.

What is Passive Listening?

The project manager must provide coaching throughout the day. We talk about everything else that is going on, but in essence, he is employing all his skills, and this is what coaching entails. If the conflicts are handled well, we reach the Norming stage.

3. Norming

In the norming phase, team members begin to work together and adjust their work habits and behaviors to support the team. The team learns to trust each other. Conflict may still arise, but the team starts to accept each other.

Everything is currently returning to normal. Productivity is increasing, and the project manager is finally acting as a mentor. He is coaching them and assisting them as needed until the team member achieves the optimal stage.

4. Performing

Performing is the stage that all project managers should ideally achieve. Teams that reach the performing stage function as a well-organized unit. They are interdependent and work through issues smoothly and effectively. Everyone on the team is free to perform what they do best. As a project manager, you take a step back and let the team do their work. If you continue to push them after they reach this point, the team will not function and will not ever develop. You must allow the team to progress during the performance phase. Once the team has completed the performing stage, the final stage will then begin.

5. Adjourning

In the adjourning phase, the team completes the work and moves on from the project. This typically occurs when staff is released from the project as deliverables are completed or as part of carrying out the Close Project or Phase process. The project manager must act as a servant leader throughout the entire journey, and that is one crucial hat we need to wear as a project manager. We must meet the requirements for the teams' training.

Journey of Training

- Team and individual training requirements
- Conduct training.
- Evaluate training results.
- Present the team member with a certificate.

Emotional Intelligence

Emotional intelligence is credited to Daniel Goldman as its founder. Daniel Goldman claims that it involves comprehending the other person's feelings and way of thinking. Emotional intelligence consists of five main domains:-

1. Understand yourself

As Confucius said, know yourself by understanding yourself.

- Becoming aware of oneself.
- What brings you joy?
- What makes you happy?
- What does not make you happy?

- Other people can take advantage of you if you do not understand yourself.
- You could end up acting as their puppet if other individuals use the triggers whenever they please.

2. Manage yourself

What is the use of knowing oneself if you cannot control yourself accordingly?

3. Social skills

Social skills have two parts.

- Understanding other people's perspectives
- Influencing others

As a project manager, you will spend 90% of your time communicating, and since you will be a communicator throughout your life, social skills will be critical to your success.

4. Empathy

- Sensitivity to other people's feelings what their feelings are. Putting oneself in their position out of sympathy. Both types of empathy— are critical.
- Inward comprehension of oneself
- External awareness of how others are feeling.

5. Motivation

Understanding the motivation behind a conflict is one of the most crucial things a project manager can do whenever one arises. How motivation works in people. The rest of knowing what drives people.

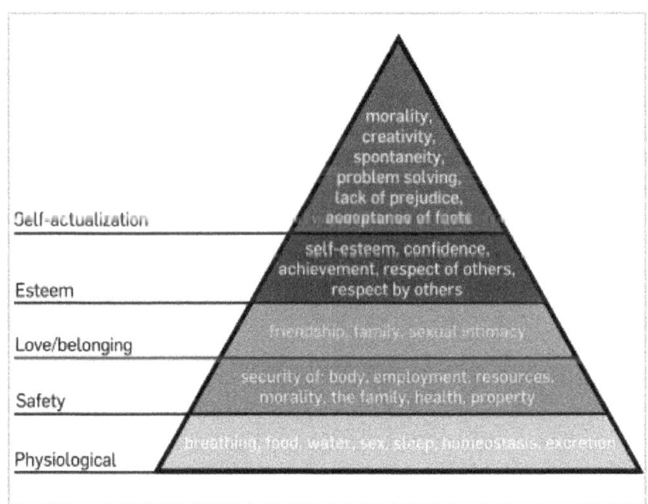

[Reference: Research Gate Maslow's Need Hierarchy (Maslow, 1943)]

Abraham Maslow's Hierarchy of Needs.

There are several ideas about motivation, with Abraham Maslow's hierarchy of needs being the first and most significant. According to Maslow, there are various levels of needs and wants, and if the lesser needs are not met, you will not even consider the higher demands.

Physiological Needs

Breathing, food, water, and safety. Once our physiological needs are met, we turn to our desires for protection.

- **Safety Needs**
  Home, money, bank balance, exercise, and health are followed by a focus on love and belonging.

- **Love/Belonging**
  We want to be in a relationship and find out who loves us before moving on to self-actualization from a place of self-worth.

Herzberg's Two Factor Theory

Federick Herzberg, an American Psychologist, proposed the Two Factor Theory after conducting a study that included 200 employees from nine different companies. The theory states that two factors or needs must be fulfilled to motivate the employees to perform better. These factors are independent of each other and thus affect behaviors differently. Herzberg's theory is also known as the motivation-hygiene theory.

- Motivating Agent
- Hygiene Agent

a) Motivating Agents

Herzberg mentions several motivational factors in this theory. Responsibility, growth, recognition, self-development promotion and other such opportunities are the primary motivating factors concerning a job. The factors act as job enrichment elements and are also known as motivators.

b) Hygiene Agents

Herzberg also identified hygiene factors related to the work, such as company policies, salary, and the physical environment. If hygiene factors are insufficient, they cause dissatisfaction. However, their presence will not motivate the employees to work better.

1. Expectancy Theory

The expectation theory, often known as the vroom theory, contends that we accomplish what we anticipate. If we think that this will be helpful, we act accordingly. We will not do that if we anticipate it will not be of any significance. The foundation of any religion is the expectation hypothesis.

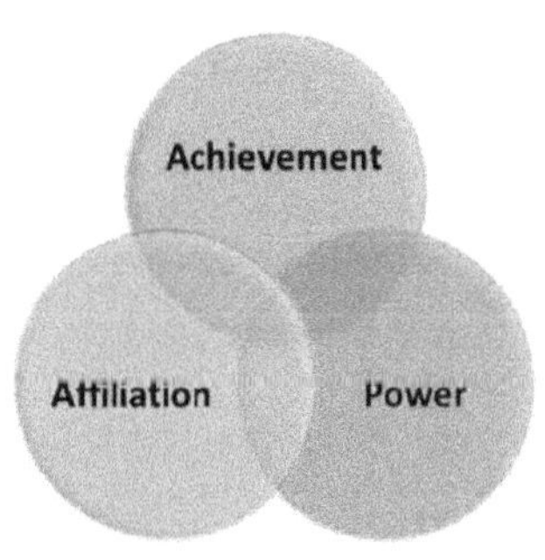

2. Theory X and Theory Y

Theory X and Theory Y are the main ways management functions in the real world. Theory X deal with the fact that because people do not enjoy their jobs, we must constantly keep an eye on them.

3. Macklin's Theory of Achievement

Macklin said that there are three elements,

- Power
- Achievement
- Affiliation

The combination of these three also motivates people. Power and a mixture of them can be used to motivate people, however some people are simply driven by these two factors, while others are driven by affiliation, achievement, and power.

Conflict Management

Conflict is inevitable in a project environment. Sources of conflict include scarce resources, scheduling priorities, and personal work styles. Team ground rules, group norms, and solid project management practices, like communication planning and role definition, reduce the amount of conflict.

The project managers must determine the level or stage of the conflict— referred to as the conflict's stage, to manage it. There are five conflict phases.

1. Problem to Solve

At this point, the team is cooperating and directing all its discussions towards the issue.

- They are accepting ideas and working to find a solution.
- They are talking about ways to fix the issue.
- We are discussing the facts rather than pointing the finger at anyone, and the language is open.

- If the project manager notices that we have a problem to fix, he never gets involved. Let the group figure it out. Let the group develop. Let the group grow.

2. Disagreement

The squad members are at odds with one another. If the issue is not resolved at this point, it moves on to dispute. At this stage, the blame game begins. The project manager must intervene at this point, stage two, before the issue escalates to context.

3. Contest

We are no longer interested in the conflict at this point.

4. Crusade

Conflict moves to crusade if it is still not resolved at contest level. We have evolved into becoming ideological now. We are discussing ideology. We are not discussing a concern.

5. World War

The members of the team at this stage cannot even look at one another. The team must be isolated by the project manager to determine how to address the situation. Chances are, they could start abusing each other or become nasty towards one another. In this case, separate the team members and allow the situation to calm down, as in a world war. Use diplomacy at the crusade level. At the contest level, strive to keep the overall picture in mind. Try to identify the problem's underlying causes and demonstrate to the participants how problem-solving can help with this agreement. When they get there, let them handle their own problem-solving. Explain why the situation happened.

To resolve disagreement, contest, crusade, and world war, we must de-escalate the situation from one of its five stages. There are three phases to solving any issue or identifying its source.

- Determine the nature of the issue.
- Identify various solutions- whatever the solution is. Choose a solution - Adopt it, modify it, replace it, and select an alternative if the current one is ineffective.

Conflict Management Techniques

Successful conflict management results in greater productivity and positive working relationships. When managed properly, differences of opinion can lead to increased creativity and better decision making. If the differences become a negative factor, project team members are initially responsible for their resolution. If conflict escalates, the project manager should help facilitate a satisfactory resolution. Conflict should be addressed early and usually in private, using a direct, collaborative approach. If disruptive conflict continues, formal procedures may be used, including disciplinary actions. The success of project managers in managing their project teams often depends a great deal on their ability to resolve conflict. Different project managers may utilize different conflict resolution methods. Factors that influence conflict resolution methods include:

- Relative importance and intensity of the conflict,
- Time pressure for resolving the conflict,
- Position of persons involved, and
- Motivation to resolve conflict on a long-term or a short-term basis.

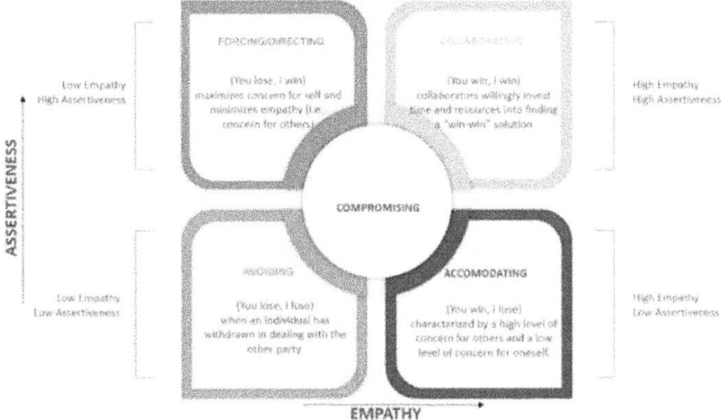

[Reference: Quality Gurus Conflict Resolution Model]

There are five general techniques for resolving conflict. As each one has its place and use, these are not given in any order:

1. Collaborate/Problem Solve.

Incorporating multiple viewpoints and insights from differing perspectives; requires a cooperative attitude and open dialogue that typically leads to consensus and commitment. Seeking to create a win-win scenario.

2. Smooth/Accommodate.

Emphasizing areas of agreement rather than areas of difference; conceding one's position to the needs of others to maintain harmony and relationships. Smoothing and accommodating are useful when reaching the overarching goal is more important than the disagreement.

3. Force/Direct.

Pushing one's viewpoint at the expense of others; offering only win-lose solutions, usually enforced through a power position to resolve an emergency. In this situation, other feelings take precedence over your own. Forcing is used when there is not enough time to collaborate or problem-solve.

4. Withdraw/Avoid.

Retreating from an actual or potential conflict situation; postponing the issue to be better prepared or to be resolved by others. Avoid this lose-lose situation at all costs or withdraw. Here, you try to avoid the issue. You simply record. You do not do anything about it.

5. Compromise/Reconcile.

There are some conflicts in which all parties will not be fully satisfied. In those instances, finding a way to compromise is the best approach. Compromise entails a willingness to give and take. This allows all parties to get something they want, and it avoids escalating the conflict. This style is often used when the parties involved have equal "power."

Resource Management Plan

The resource management plan provides guidance on how project human resources should be defined, staffed, managed, and eventually released. It can also contain roles and responsibilities, project organization charts, and the staffing management plan, which form a key input to identify risk process.

There are four **types of resources,**

- Manpower
- Machinery
- Money
- Material

Resource management plan will define,

- Who will do?
- What will do?

- Where will do?
- When will do?

RAM (Responsibility Assignment Matrix)

A Responsibility Assignment Matrix (RAM) is a project management tool that maps out project tasks against the people responsible for them. It is a grid that shows the project resources assigned to each work package. The RAM is used to depict the relationship between work to be done and project team members. It is a useful tool for clarifying roles and responsibilities in a project and ensuring that everyone knows what they are responsible for.

	Project Manager	Engineering Manager	Quality Assurance Manager	Purchasing Manager	Manufacturing Manager
Create blueprints	A	R	C		C
Manufacture circuit board	I	A	C		R
Test circuit board	I	R	A		C
Order components	C	C	I	R	A
Assemble	I	C	C		R

RACI is an extension of the RAM matrix. It is a common way of showing stakeholders who are responsible, accountable, consulted, or informed and are associated with project activities, decisions, and deliverables.

- Responsibility- Who is responsible to do something?
- Accountable- Who is accountable to do something?
- Consult- Whom to consult?
- Inform- Whom to inform?

Resource Calendar

A resource calendar is a tool used in project management to keep track of the working days and non-working days of the project team members. It helps the project manager to assign tasks to team members based on their availability. The resource calendar lists all the working days, holidays, and other non-working days of the team members. By using the resource calendar, the project manager can ensure that the team members are available to work when needed to execute the project tasks.

Recognition and Rewards

Part of the team development process involves recognizing and rewarding desirable behavior. It is important to recognize that a particular reward given to any individual will be effective only if it satisfies a need which is valued by that individual. Award decisions are made, formally or informally, during the process of managing the project team through project performance appraisals. Setting clear criteria for rewards and a planned system for their use help promote and reinforce desired behaviors. To be effective, recognition and rewards should be based on activities and performance under a person's control.

Creating a plan with established times for distribution of rewards ensures that recognition takes place and is not forgotten. The project manager must be aware of the kinds of cultures, rewards, and organizations that permit. The awards and recognition must be offered in accordance with respect to a particular area's or domain's culture. The working atmosphere needs to be extremely healthy when discussing cultures or teams, especially agile teams. It is the responsibility of the project manager to create such an environment. When someone makes a mistake, they are not dismissed, they receive favorable treatment. They are handled in a way that benefits the businesses. Provide a decent working atmosphere so that people can learn from their mistakes.

I-Type Leader

I type leader have an in-depth knowledge of one domain. They are expert in one area, while lacking expertise in other areas outside their domain.

General Type Leader

A general type of leader is one who is knowledgeable about everything but lacks a niche.

T-Type Leader

I-type and General type leaders are combined to create T-type leaders. People who are deeply knowledgeable about one domain and are also knowledgeable about other areas are called T-Type leaders.

PRACTICE EXAM QUESTIONS

Question 1

Your team has been arguing with each other for last two weeks, however now they understand habits of each other and start working together at which stage your team is.

A. Performing
B. Smoothing
C. Norming
D. Forming
E. Storming

Correct answer

C – Norming

Question 2

Two team members having been discussing how to solve the problem what should the project manager do.

A. Take part in argument and find a solution.
B. Do nothing.
C. Escalate issue to HR.
D. Talk to function manager about team members.

Correct Answer

B – Do nothing.

Question 3

Team members have been fighting for two weeks, project manager came and listened both parties and then he decided, both parties must give up on this decision, which conflict management technique is this.

A. Smoothing

B. Problem solving
C. Accommodating
D. Compromising

Correct Answer

D – Compromising

Question 4

You are working in an agile team, a team member comes to you and share he is unable to do complex analysis, as a project manager what will you do.

A. Arrange training for the team.
B. Report him to HR.
C. Arrange coaching for him.
D. Put the issue in issue log.

Correct answer

A – Arrange coaching for him.

Question 5

You have geographically distributed team all the world, while in standup you have noticed, sometime some team members are smoking, some team members are eating and sometimes there is a background noise behind team members which is causing issue in complete team what will you do to handle these issues.

A. Report this issue to ethical violation committee.
B. Do nothing implement ground rules to stop these things.
C. A list of work teams to be completed in the next sprint.
D. Accept this as new normal.

Correct Answer

B – Do nothing implement ground rules to stop these things

5. AGILE

Agile

Agile is an iterative methodology for managing projects and creating software that speeds up time to value for consumers. An agile team avoids risky "big bang" launches in favor of more frequent, smaller, and more manageable product releases. Continuous evaluation of requirements, plans, and results gives teams a built-in way to adapt to new circumstances.

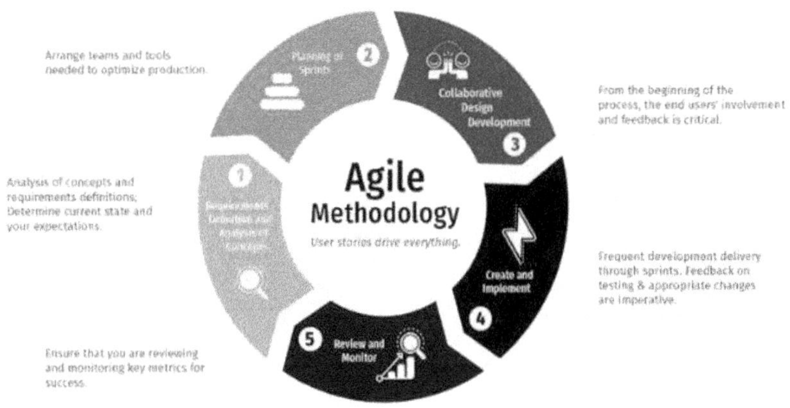

[Reference: Nvisia Agile Methodology]

Agile Manifesto

<u>**The four values of the agile manifesto:**</u>

1. **Individuals and interactions over processes and tools**

While traditional project management often relies heavily on following established processes and using specific tools to manage the project, the agile project management prioritizes the importance of people and communication. In this approach, the project team works closely together, collaborating and communicating regularly to ensure that everyone is on the same page and working towards the same goals. This allows for greater flexibility and adaptability, as the team can adjust, and changes as needed to ensure that the project is successful.

2. **Working software over comprehensive documentation**

The concept of "working software over comprehensive documentation" works by prioritizing the delivery of a working product to the customer, rather than focusing solely on creating extensive documentation.

In agile project management, the project team works closely with the customer to understand their needs and preferences. The team then develops the product iteratively, with regular feedback and testing. This approach allows for greater flexibility and adaptability, as the team can adjust, and changes as needed to ensure that the final product meets the customer's expectations.

3. **Customer collaboration over contract negotiation**

The concept of "customer collaboration over contract negotiation" is a key principle of agile project management. It emphasizes the importance of working closely with the customer throughout the project to understand their needs and preferences, rather than relying on a rigid contract to define the project's scope and requirements. This approach allows for greater flexibility and adaptability and can help ensure that the project delivers value to the customer and meets their needs. It also allows for greater creativity and innovation, as the team can explore innovative ideas and approaches in collaboration with the customer. Overall, the concept of "customer collaboration over contract negotiation" is a key aspect of the agile methodology and can help organizations achieve greater success in their projects.

4. **Responding to change over following a plan.**

The concept of "responding to change over following a plan" is a fundamental principle of the agile methodology. Unlike traditional project management, which relies on a rigid change control procedure, agile project management allows for greater flexibility and adaptability. In agile, there is no change control board. Instead, any change requests are directed to the product owner, who evaluates the request and determines its priority. The request is then added to the product backlog and prioritized based on its value and risk. The team then works to incorporate the change request into the next sprint, ensuring that it is completed in a timely and efficient manner.

What Really Is Agile?

It has 4 Core Values:

- Individuals and interactions over processes and tools
- Working software over comprehensive documentation
- Customer collaboration over contract negotiation
- Responding to a changeover following a plan

The 12 Principles of Agile

1. Satisfy the customer- highest priority.
2. Welcome change.
3. Deliver Frequently-deliver whatever the frequency is.
4. Work Together-maximum 12 team members.
5. Trust and Support
6. Face-to-face conversations
7. Working software
8. Sustainable Development
9. Continuous Attention
10. Maintaining simplicity

11. Self-organizing team
12. Reflect and Adjust

The following agile principle i.e., working together, trust support, face-to-face conversation and self-organizing is all about the team.

T- type

T-type mean people have expertise in one domain but also have an idea about other domains so that there are fewer points of failure. We prefer to have face-to-face conversations, but this principle will be updated soon because now increased people are working from home and all the companies are supporting this method. The team must be self-organized. In agile, we want to have sustainable progress. It does not mean we do one thing for 12 hours and then we do not do anything at all.

12 Principles of Agile in Software Development

1. Early delivery of the project
2. Adapt to change.
3. Frequent Delivery
4. Business and Developer cooperation
5. Motivated individuals
6. Face-to-face interaction
7. Working software
8. Maintain a constant pace.
9. Technical brilliance
10. Simplicity
11. Self-organizing team
12. Regular reflection and adjustment

In Rolling Wave Planning, we first plan at a high level and then as we move forward, we keep on re-planning. As more detail comes, we expand on the details. How do we do that? When we are talking about agile planning we plan at multiple levels.

The 5 Levels of Agile Planning

[Reference: Project Manager Interview Questions: The 5 levels in Agile planning]

Agile is a project management methodology that is designed to cater to environments with **constantly changing requirements and goals**. This means that the traditional planning model, which involves setting everything in motion at the beginning of the project, is no longer viable.

To implement agile, there are several key planning stages that must be followed. The first stage is to create a **product vision**, which defines the project's purpose and goals. The second stage is to create a **product roadmap**, which outlines the steps that need to be taken to achieve the product vision. The roadmap is made up of all the required features, which are prioritized based on their importance and represent how the product will be built.

The next stage of planning is the **release plan**, which defines how many releases the product will have. The release plan is not focused on features or dates, but rather on the scope of work to be completed.

Sprints, also known as iterations, are the next stage of planning. Sprint planning is done more frequently and relates to the day-to-day tasks of each employee. It is a flexible planning event that allows the team to react to any changes in requirements and circumstances and move forward to project completion.

The final stage of agile planning is the **daily stand-up**, which is a 15-minute meeting held daily in the same place and location. The stand-up is a planning event that defines the goals for the next day and involves discussing the following three questions.

1. What have you done yesterday?
2. What are you going to do today?
3. Is there an impediment or roadblock?

Scrum Framework

Scrum is one of the most popular Agile frameworks originally used for developing software projects. Scrum is characterized by fixed time iterations called sprints which usually last 2-4 weeks. At the end of the sprint, all team members discuss further planning.

The scrum framework is the thing in the scrum that we can see and work. The following three roles makes up the scrum team.

- Product owner

The product owner is the voice of the customer. He is your organization's team member, but he is the person who understands the product best. You can consider him a business analyst. He will be the person who will be deciding on what would the product look like and how you can work.

- Development team

The development team decides how the work will be done and what work will be done.

- Scrum master

We do not have a project manager in the scrum; we have a scrum master. He does not have the same authority or responsibility as a project manager, but he is there to make sure that we follow the entire scrum framework and proper procedure.

Events in Scrum

1- Sprint

Sprint has a duration of one to four weeks and at the end of a sprint, you must make something that the customer needs to have.

2- Sprint Planning

In sprint planning, we plan for the sprint. What we are going to do, what are the things in the sprint? As a result of sprint planning, we get a sprint backlog. The things that you are going to produce in this sprint as well as you also make sprint goals that you share with the customer.

3- Daily Stand-up

It is also called a stand-up or scrum meeting. The duration of daily stand-up is 15 minutes, and it is fixed. The purpose of daily stand-up is to inspect what has been done and adopt the change to work accordingly. You ask only three questions:

- What have you done yesterday?
- What are you going to do today?
- Is there any impediment, roadblocks, or problems?

It is for the team, by the team. The scrum master is there to make sure that we end the meeting within 15 minutes.

4- **Sprint Review**

In sprint review, the product owner, customer, sponsor, team, and scrum master everyone come and look at the work. The requirements are called user stories. In the sprint review, there are two things. If the product owner accepts it, it goes into the product increment and becomes a part of the final solution. If it gets rejected, it can be because of two reasons:

1. It is not completed, and we do not even show it to the customer.
2. It just does not meet the agreed requirement.

Whatever the case, if it is not complete as per the agreed work or it is rejected, it goes back into the product backlog. At the end of two weeks, the sprint is over. There is no further discussion on sprint. Whatever is completed goes into the product increment and whatever is incomplete or rejected goes into the product backlog.

This is where new user stories are added, and the product backlog is reprioritized as high value and high risk and it is re-prioritized. We also refer to it as grooming of product backlog.

5- Sprint Retrospective

The sprint retrospective is a key event in the agile methodology that takes place at the end of each sprint. It provides an opportunity for the project team to reflect on the sprint that has just been completed and identify areas for improvement. During the retrospective, the team discusses what went well, what did not go well, and what could be improved in the future. The goal of the sprint retrospective is to help the team continuously improve and refine their processes, leading to greater success in future sprints.

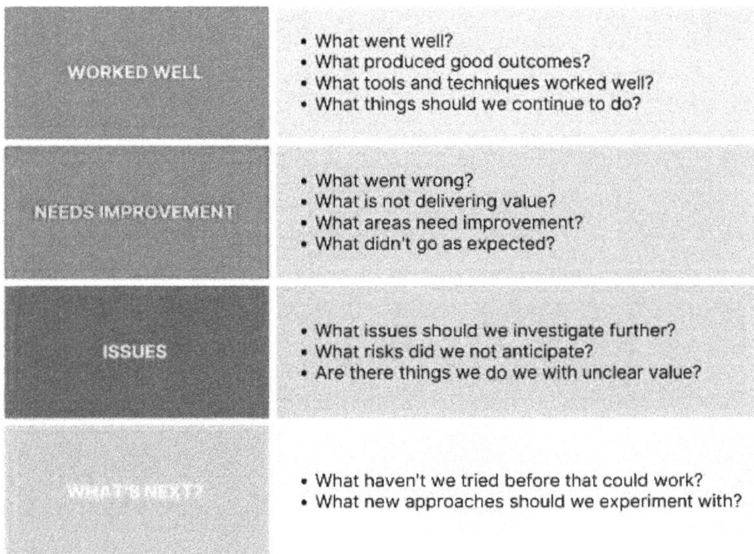

The sprint retrospective is an important part of the agile methodology, as it encourages collaboration and communication among team members and provides a structured way to reflect on past performance and identify areas for improvement.

1. **Set the stage**

The scrum master is the facilitator. He sets the stage, like what we are going to expect and what is happening. He shares those things with every single person; he clarifies the requirements – what we are going to do set the stage.

2. **Gather Data**

We get the data from every person, and we look at the entire sprint what has been done.

3. **Generate Insight**

Here we are doing root cause analysis. We are trying to see what is done well or badly and how we can improve.

4. **Decide on improvements**

We decide on improvements.

5. **Close the Retrospective**

We close by thanking each other for attending.

The product backlog is the list of all the requirements. The requirements are in the form of a user story. A user story, the syntax of the user story is as a user, Hey coach (defining who you are), I want to make this pathway series (requirement) so that I can teach more people (criteria) through the live YouTube videos. You put down all the requirements into the product backlog on sticky notes. Each user story follows 3 C's.

They are written on the cards like sticky notes. There is a conversation on the cards and on the back side, there are confirmation criteria. Each user story must follow the acronym of INVEST.

INDEPENDENT - They must be independent of each other. One user story should not depend on another.

NEGOTIABLE - they must be negotiable like you must be able to negotiate such that there should be no user story that becomes a showstopper.

VALUABLE - They should provide value to the customer.

ESTIMATABLE - You must be able to estimate them estimable.

SMALL - they should be small like you can complete them in one sprint. The user stories that you cannot complete in one sprint are big user stories we call them epic.

TESTABLE - User stories must be testable – you must be able to test them.

The product owner goes to all the stakeholders. He collects their requirements. All the user stories a, b, c, d, and e take all the requirements. He puts all the requirements into the product backlog – one place for all the requirements. We get the product backlog. Once all requirements are there, it goes back to the stakeholders which can be customers, sponsors or whomever it is and asks them, let us rate this as high value. Which of them is of the highest value and they rate them through the high value then if the needed team can also come and the team can rate here which of the requirement has higher risk because the team knows the work high value, high risk. The product backlog is prioritized by high-value, high–risk, high–value, and medium-risk.

BACKLOG PRIORITIZATION TECHNIQUES

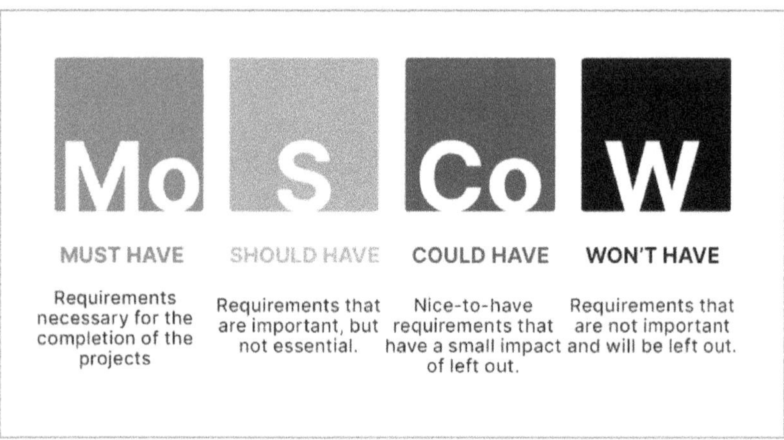

Following are a few techniques that are used to prioritize the product backlog.

MOSCOW

The MoSCoW method is a four-step approach to prioritizing which project requirements provide the best return on investment (ROI). MoSCoW stands for must have, should have, could have, and will not have -- the o's make the acronym more pronounceable.

- M- What are the MUST requirement?
- S-What are the SHOULD requirements?
- C-What are the COULD requirements?
- W-What are the WILL NOT HAVE requirement?

100 Points Technique.

In this technique, we give 100 points to the stakeholder, and they prioritize them on each user's story and then we count the points whichever user story has more points becomes the highest prioritized user story. Once we have the product backlog ready, the team will next estimate that requirement using agile methodology, such as lightweight estimate.

In agile we refer to it as **ideal hours** as we are considering that all the time we will spend working will not actually happen. Whenever you estimate in ideal hours you always get more time into that so that is the least usable technique for estimation there are three estimation techniques for each user story.

Affinity Estimation

Affinity means categorizing since agile is a knowledge work, we do not know exactly most of the time how much it will take but we can compare each user story with others for example we say this is a small user story this is a medium, large, XL or XXL, many organizations still use affinity estimation.

Fibonacci Series Estimation.

Fibonacci states that as your user story size increases the complexity gets more and so the team says this user story is two-story point four-story point five eight etc. , whatever the team says only the team knows what two mean what does five mean so you cannot compare the story points of one team with the other team. Story point is the effort required to complete a user story, so one-story point effort is one two means two-three means three efforts.

Planning Poker

In planning poker, the team sits in a circle, and the scrum master explains the user story that needs to be covered in the product backlog. The team then counts to three and simultaneously reveals their estimates for the story point. If there is a difference in the estimates, the scrum master asks the team members to explain their reasoning. The team then plays planning poker again until a consensus is reached.

Wideband Delphi

Wideband alpha is another technique that can be used to achieve consensus. In this technique, the team members discuss the user story and their estimates, and then the estimates are averaged to arrive at a consensus estimate.

Both planning poker and wideband alpha are effective techniques for achieving consensus among team members and ensuring that everyone is on the same page. By using these techniques, the team can work together more effectively and efficiently, leading to greater success in the project.

Next, we start sprint planning, here the team tells how many stories points they can complete in one sprint. It is important to remember that Agile teams are self-organized, nobody but the team will decide how much work they can complete in one sprint, which is referred to as the velocity of the sprint.

Velocity is the number of stories points you can complete in one sprint and story points are the effort required to complete the user story so that becomes the velocity of a sprint.

You get a sprint backlog here once we gain the agreement between the product owner and the team on what user story should be there and what should not be there, once the agreement is reached, we start working on those user stories, so this is **sprint backlog/product backlog**.

Then we have product increment as the user stories are completed, they are added as an increment in the document this is completed, we add them so that is called **product increment** so that is the entire thing you need to know about the scrum.

The product backlog is approved by the product owner because he has already taken the requirements from the sponsors so now you can say that sponsor approves the product backlog but normally product owner is responsible for the product backlog.

Lean is all about waste removal, whenever you hear the word lean understand this means the elimination of waste. Therefore, in lean we make use of a tool known as value stream mapping where we map the entire workflow based on the value-added tasks. We define the known value-added tasks, categorize them by efficient value-added tasks over the total time.

Kanban Method

As described by the Agile Alliance, the Kanban Method is focused on designing, managing, and improving flow systems for knowledge work. It holds transparency, balance, collaboration, flow, and leadership among its values, though there are other characteristics as well.

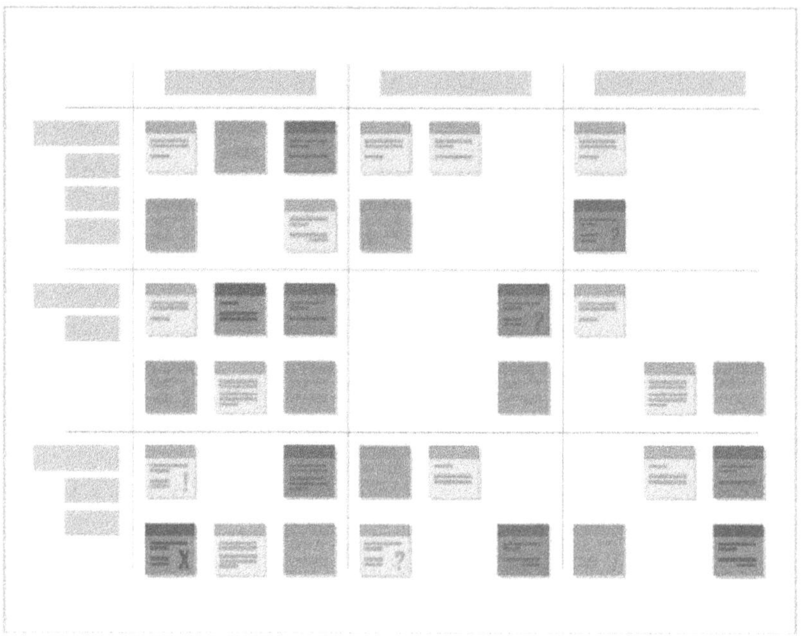

Kanban is a visual system that leads to work management by visualizing the workflow and actual work. The primary goal is to identify obstacles that may occur in the development journey and subsequently resolve them. The method evolved out of a response to various challenges faced by other agile methods, precisely Scrum. This method is opposite to that of a non-disruptive evolutionary method. In addition, it helps to deliver the product continuously instead of a time duration of 2 to 3 weeks. This results in a much quicker turnaround.

Extreme Programming (XP)

Also known as **pair programming** is another software development framework that lists its goal as wanting to produce higher quality software and higher quality of life for the development team. In XP, two team members sit together and do pair programming one by one. One person codes while the other checks, so they can immediately tackle the issue if there is a problem.

The general characteristics of XP are:

- Dynamically changing software requirements
- Risks caused by fixed-time projects using new technology.
- The small, co-located extended development team.
- The technology you are using allows for automated unit and functional tests.

In the context of Extreme Programming (XP), there are several important terms to be aware of. One such term is technical debt, which refers to the accumulation of problems that arise when code is not simplified and is continually added to without proper refactoring. Refactoring is the process of simplifying code without changing its original functionality. By refactoring regularly, technical debt can be minimized, and the codebase can be kept clean and maintainable.

XP is recommended for projects that have high changing requirements

Feature Driven Development

The Feature Driven Development framework focuses on large teams working with short iterations. The goal is to facilitate the delivery of features in a short period of time.

The project has 5 stages under the FDD framework, putting the individual features front and center. The initial three stages are sequential — these are the "develop an overall model," "build a features list," and "plan by feature" stages. The final two stages — "design by feature" and "build by feature" — are interactive.

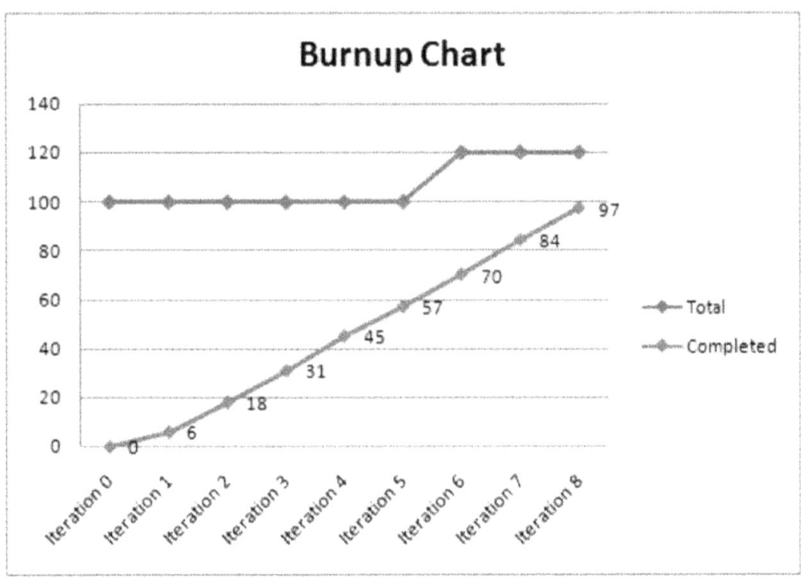

In FDD, there are various activities that assist teammates in addressing communication challenges and coordinating better. It has found particular use in large organizations but is not often used for smaller projects.

What Is Sprint Zero?

In Scrum, before starting the first sprint or iteration, there is a preliminary stage known as sprint zero. During this stage, an architectural spike is performed to establish proof of concept and determine whether the project can be successfully executed. This spike is focused on testing the feasibility of the project and ensuring that the team has a clear understanding of the technical requirements.

In contrast, a risk spike is a special user story that is focused on mitigating potential risks associated with the project. Unlike an architectural spike, a risk spike does not involve any work related to product development. Instead, the team focuses solely on identifying and addressing potential risks that could impact the success of the project.

Both architectural and risk spikes are important components of the Scrum methodology, as they help to ensure that the project is executed successfully and that potential risks are identified and addressed early on. By performing these spikes during sprint zero, the team can establish a solid foundation for the project and set themselves up for success in future sprints.

Information Radiators refers to the burnup chart and burn-down chart.

Burndown Chart

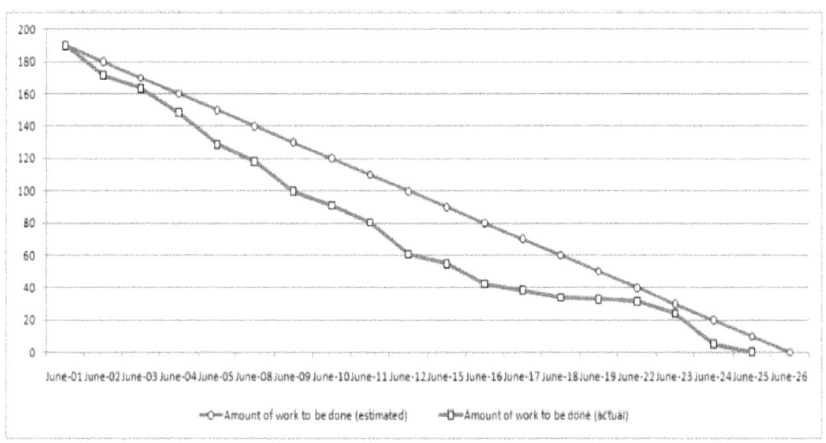

The Burndown chart is a data representation and analysis technique that tracks the amount of work remaining on a project, or the remaining effort, as the project progresses. It provides a visual representation of the team's progress and can be used to determine whether the team is on track to meet their goals.

Another useful tool in project management is the Task board, which is a simple board that represents the status of the work, including to-do, in progress, and completed. A variation of the Task board is the Kanban board, which can be used to track lead time and cycle time.

Lead time refers to the time between when a user story is requested and when it is approved for completion. In the Kanban board, lead time is measured from the time the user story is requested until it is completed.

Cycle time, on the other hand, is the time between when the team starts working on a user story and when it is completed. Both lead time and cycle time are important metrics that project teams strive to decrease to improve project efficiency and success.

The Hybrid Approach

It is important to remember that Agile is a mindset, and no project is entirely Agile or predictive by nature. Instead, most projects are a combination of both, which is known as a hybrid approach.

For example, while following agile principles on a project, it may be necessary to conduct procurements through a predictive approach, and vice versa. This hybrid approach allows for greater flexibility and adaptability, as the project team can adjust, and changes as needed to ensure that the final product meets the customer's needs and expectations. By embracing a hybrid approach, the project team can achieve greater success in their projects by leveraging the strengths of both Agile and predictive methodologies.

PRACTICE EXAM QUESTIONS

Question 1

You are the project manager of IT project. You are in last sprint, and customer has asked you to add a new requirement what would you do.

A. A change request.
B. Update stakeholder engagement plan
C. Add new requirement to product backlog.
D. Talk to product owner and inform him about requirement.

Correct answer.

D – Talk to product owner and inform him about requirement.

Question 2

When does sprint ends?

A. When all the items are sprint backlog get completed
B. When time is over
C. When product owner says it is over
D. When customer decide to end it

Correct answer.

B – When time is over

Question 3

You are the scrum master, you are facilitating, and team member are discussing and planning in detail about risk, what is wrong in this meeting.

A. Nothing, this is the purpose of standup meeting.
B. Product owner is missing.
C. Customer also needs to be in this meeting.

D. Daily standup is only for progress.

Correct Answer

D – Daily standup is only for progress.

Question 4

You are a scrum master on a five-person co-located software team. In the most recent retrospective, someone on your team suggested that the team might be overloaded with too much work in progress. What is the BEST thing for you to do?

A. Tell the team to finish the work within the sprint.
B. Tell the customers to funnel all requests through you so the team does not get overloaded.
C. Experiment with setting WIP limits
D. All of the above

Correct answer

C – Experiment with setting WIP limits

Question 5

Paul is a developer on an agile software team. During a planning session, the product owner tells everyone that customer have asked for performance improvements in their upcoming release. Performance problems have caused a few cancellations recently and the situation is quickly becoming a priority for many customers. What should the team do next?

A. Prioritize the performance improvement toward the top the sprint backlog so the team focuses on it.
B. Create the persona for the user who request the feature.
C. Add the feature request to the product backlog for later consideration.

D. Create a non-functional requirements document and inside the performance requirements in it.

Correct answer

A – Prioritize the performance improvement toward the top the sprint backlog so the team focuses on it.

6.RISK

Risk Management

Risk refers to an uncertain event that has the potential to either positively or negatively impact a project. There is always a level of uncertainty associated with risks, as it is impossible to predict with complete accuracy whether they will occur. This uncertainty can make it difficult to plan for and manage risks, as there is always a chance that they may have a negative impact on the project. However, by identifying and assessing risks, project teams can take steps to mitigate their potential impact and increase the likelihood of project success.

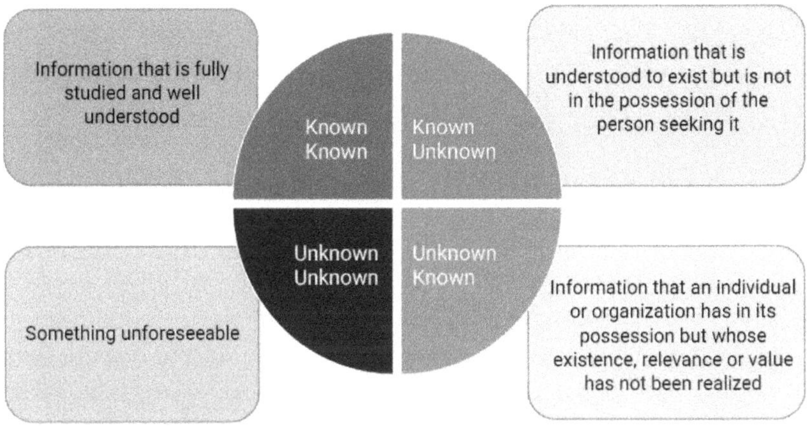

Overview of Risk Management

Risk management is a critical component of an organizational culture that values prudent risk-taking. It involves a systematic process of identifying, assessing, and responding to risks, and communicating the outcomes of these processes to relevant parties in a timely manner.

Depending on the governance structure, once the risk management strategy is developed, approval is obtained from the sponsor, the organization, and the change control board. After the strategy has been authorized, the process of identifying risks can begin. The question then arises as to how to recognize risks, which is not a strict order as anything could come first or last.

The project manager typically reviews project documents such as the project management plan, project scope statement, and the OPAS. The project manager also consults with sponsors and other key stakeholders to determine which risks are most crucial and establish a risk management plan based on the organization's risk appetite. The identified risks are then agreed upon and prioritized based on the risk tolerance. All risks are entered into the risk register and monitored until they are closed.

Let us understand few risks related keywords before we dive deeper into the topic.

1) Probability.

It might be low, medium, or high depending on the organization, or it can be extremely low, low, medium, high, or very high. It is interesting to note that each company has its own concept of what the terms "low," "high," and "extremely high" mean in this context. This likelihood may be minimal for one organization while it may be high for another with identical objectives.

2) Impact

Impact is crucial from the perspective of the organization. One million is an extremely high-risk number for some organizations, either in a positive or negative way. For large enterprises, one million dollars is nothing, thus the organization's risk management plan defines what is high, what is medium, and what is low, i.e., the impact of the risk.

3) Risk Averse

When an organization is risk-averse, it means that they avoid it because they see risk as a bad thing. The organization's life and budget significantly influence how it will approach a certain risk because if the organization is more established, like the government agency, it will become risk averse as it attempts to avoid the risk.

4) Risk Seeker

Risk seeker are businesses that actively seek out risk. When a company or individual is young, they are more risk-takers and desire to take the danger head-on.

5) Risk neutral

The company calculates the risk's positive and negative impacts, and based on those impacts, they determine the risk associated with each individual risk-related activity before calculating that specific risk.

6) RIsk Threshold/Tolerance of the organization

The threshold represents the upper bound on the amount of risk that your organization can tolerate. **Tolerance** gives us the range plus minus. For example, ± 5% you can use both threshold and tolerance.

7) Risk appetite of the organization

Appetite is the amount of risk your company is ready to accept in exchange for the potential return.

8) Risk Exposure

The overall risk of the company, or the risk that it is willing to accept.

Identifying The Risks

Tools for identifying risks:

a) SWOT Analysis
b) PESTLE Analysis
c) Expert Judgment
d) Documents reviews
e) Enterprise Environmental Factors
f) Organizational Process Assets
g) Assumption and Constraints Log
h) Business Document
i) Project Charter

To determine the risk, we use the project charter, the business case, and the benefits management plan. We start by asking the sponsor and other important stakeholders before moving on to the subject-matter experts.

1. **Focus Group** gathers qualitative data and diverse perspectives from participants who have relevant knowledge or experience in risk being examined.

2. **Facilitated workshop** a technique that uses focused sessions to bring cross-functional stakeholders together to identify risks associated with the project.

3. **Documents**- The process of identifying risks is iterative; risks can arise at any time, even after the project has been completed and therefore the documents should be reviewed.

4. **Prompt List-** a PESTLE-style categorized list. What are the risks associated with political, the economical, society, technology, the legal, and the environmental?

5. **VUCA** - Volatile, Uncertain, Complex, and Ambiguous is another method we can use. To calculate the risk, we can look at a company's strengths, weaknesses, opportunities, and threats while also noting any risks that the firm is currently facing.

Risk management is not just about identifying risks themselves. Organizations need to review their risk management plan and governance systems to ensure they are delivering effective and robust risk management that fits the project's purpose.

The more risks we uncover for any business, the more risk we identify for the project. When an organization is young, its only capability is to detect potential hazards, which can be done early on because it has organizational process assets, or the OPAs. However, as the company matures it becomes increasingly difficult to detect unidentified risks.

Prioritizing The Risks

Risk prioritization is the process of evaluating and ranking risks based on their potential impact and likelihood of occurrence. It involves identifying and assessing various risks that an organization or project may face, and then determining which risks should be addressed first or given higher priority.

The purpose of risk prioritization is to allocate resources and attention to the most critical risks that could have a significant negative impact on objectives or outcomes. By prioritizing risks, organizations can focus their efforts on managing and mitigating the most important and urgent risks, while potentially accepting or monitoring lower-priority risks.

Qualitative Risk Assessment

Qualitative risk assessment is a method used to evaluate and prioritize risks based on their qualitative characteristics rather than assigning specific numerical values. It involves identifying and analyzing risks based on their potential impact and likelihood of occurrence, without quantifying them in terms of specific numbers or monetary values.

In qualitative risk assessment, risks are typically categorized into various levels or scales, such as low, medium, and high, or using a numerical scale like 1 to 5. It is particularly useful when there is limited data or when risks cannot be easily quantified. However, it does not provide precise numerical values or probabilities, which may be necessary for certain types of analysis or decision-making. In such cases, quantitative risk assessment methods may be more appropriate.

Quantitative Risk Analysis

Quantitative risk assessment is a systematic process used to evaluate and quantify risks associated with a particular activity, project, or system. It involves the use of mathematical and statistical techniques to assign numerical values to various risk factors, such as the likelihood of an event occurring and the potential consequences of that event.

Quantitative risk assessment provides a more objective and rigorous approach to risk management by assigning numerical values to risks, allowing for better comparison and prioritization of risks. It helps decision-makers understand the potential impact of risks and make informed decisions to minimize their effects.

Tools for Quantitative Risk Analysis

1- **Influence Diagram**

The influence diagram facilitates the prioritization of tasks based on their level of importance. The tasks with higher levels of risk demand greater attention.

2- **Sensitivity Analysis / Tornado Diagram**

It rates the impact of a risk on various objectives of the project. Both positive and negative effects can be attributed to it.

3- **Expected Monetary Value (EMV)**

EMV stands for Expected Monetary Value, and it is a concept used in risk management to assess the potential financial impact of uncertain events or risks. It is a way to quantify the potential losses or gains associated with different risks.

4- **Decision Tree Analysis**

Decision tree analysis is a data mining technique used for making decisions or predictions by creating a visual representation of outcomes and their associated probabilities. It is a supervised learning algorithm that uses a tree-like structure to model decisions and their potential consequences. It is an extension of expected monetary value.

5- Monte Carlo Analysis

Monte Carlo analysis is a computational technique used to simulate and analyze complex systems or processes that involve randomness or uncertainty. Monte Carlo simulation involves using random sampling and probability distributions to model uncertain variables and their potential impact on the desired outcome. By running multiple iterations of the simulation, it generates a range of outcomes and their associated probabilities.

POSITIVE RISKS	NEGATIVE RISKS
An opportunity to improve your project.	A threat to your project's success.
Often gives improved results.	Results in a negative outcome or even failure for your project.
Should be seized and built upon.	Should be avoided, minimized, or eliminated.
Managing positive risks can include exploiting, sharing, and enhancing the risk.	Managing negative risks can include avoiding, transferring, or mitigating the risk.

Types of Risk

Positive Risk: To ensure that the risk must occur, we attempt to make both probability and impact 100% by the following responses.

- **Escalate** - Escalation is appropriate when an opportunity is outside of the project scope or when the proposed response exceeds a given manager's authority. Escalated risks are managed at the enterprise domain or other relevant part of the organization.

- **Exploit** – The exploit strategy is chosen for important opportunities that the organization wants to guarantee will be realized. This approach aims to secure the benefits of a specific opportunity by ensuring its occurrence with a 100% probability, thereby maximizing the chances of success.

- **Enhance** – The enhance strategy aims to raise the likelihood and/or significance of an opportunity. Taking early action to enhance the opportunity is usually more effective than attempting to improve its benefits after it has already arisen. By directing attention towards the causes of the opportunity, the probability of its occurrence can be increased.

- **Share** – Sharing involves transferring ownership of an opportunity to a third party so that the third-party shares some of the benefit if the opportunity occurs.

- **Accept** – Accepting an opportunity acknowledges its existence, but no proactive action is taken. This approach is suitable for low-priority opportunities and can be employed when it is impractical or not financially viable to pursue the opportunity through alternative means.

Negative Risk: To mitigate the negative threat, we try to reduce either its probability or its impact to zero by implementing the following responses.

- **Escalate** – Escalation is appropriate when a threat is outside of the portfolio, program, or project scope or when the proposed response exceeds a given manager's authority.

- **Avoid** – This involves eliminating a threat or project activity from risk impact. It may be appropriate for a high-priority threat with a high probability of occurrence.

- **Mitigate** – Risk mitigation involves implementing measures to decrease the likelihood of a threat occurring and/or minimize its potential consequences.

- **Transfer** – Transference refers to shifting the liability to third party, for example legislation, contract, and insurance.

- **Accepting –** Entails waiting for the risk to happen. We take an action if that risk occurs. There are two ways to cope with accepting risks,

Active Acceptance happens when we plan our activities around the risk.

- Contingency plan: refers to risk response strategy developed in advance before things go wrong; it is meant to be used when identified risks become reality.

- Fallback plan: refers to alternative set of actions and tasks available if the primary plan needs to be abandoned because of issues, risks, or other causes.

Passive Acceptance occurs when we identify the risk and do nothing about it.

- Management Reserves: refers to the portion of project budget that a team can use if a project encounters unknown unknowns.

The Change Control Board conducts a review of the Risk Register and Risk Response Plan upon their completion. The Sponsor provides agreement to the Risk Mitigation Strategy.

Upon approval of the plan, all associated plans, including those for Scope, Schedule, Cost, Quality, and Procurement, are updated, and a Risk Register is established.

Furthermore, weekly risk meetings are held during which Risk Reports are presented.

What Is Risk Report?

A risk report is a document that utilizes information from the risk register to provide a forecast of potential risks for a period of one to two weeks. It is important to consider the possible risks associated with this report and determine the extent to which the organization is exposed to risk. It is worth noting that every risk has a trigger, and each trigger is monitored by the assigned risk owner. Furthermore, each risk is assigned a single owner who is responsible for its oversight. After implementing the risk response strategy, however, there is a possibility of other risks arising.

1) **Residual risk** is the risk that remains after an organization has implemented all the security controls, policies, and procedures they believe are appropriate to take. It is the risk that remains after all efforts have been made to mitigate the inherent risk.
2) **Secondary risk** is a risk that arises because of the implementation of a risk response plan. It is a new risk that emerges because of the actions taken to mitigate the original risk.

What Is Risk Audit?

Risk audit is the examination and documentation of the effectiveness of risk responses in dealing with identified risk and their root causes, as well as the effectiveness of the risk management process. Throughout the project, we continue to watch out for potential risks. If a risk is identified before it materializes, it is recorded in the risk register, and operations are continued as planned.

However, if the risk necessitates a modification to the project plan, a change request must be submitted, and any contingencies for potential risks must be utilized.

Difference between Risk Vs. Issue

RISK	ISSUE
Focused on the future	Focused on the present
It can be positive or negative	Will always be negative
Documented in the Risk Register	Documented in the Issue Log
Response is called a risk response	Response is called a workaround

Difference between Risk Management Plan Vs. Risk Register

RISK MANAGEMENT PLAN	RISK REGISTER
Definition of identified risks.	List of all the prioritized risks
Tolerance of organization	Establishes potential risk response
Stakeholder Appetite	Risk owner

PRACTICE EXAM QUESTIONS

Question 1

You are working in a construction project, you have made risk management plan, identified risk both qualitatively and quantitatively, planned their response, you have assigned risk owner to monitor all the risk. You got a call last night from your team that unidentified risk has occurred in the project. As a project manager what will you do first?

A. Escalate to sponsor.
B. Put the risk in the risk register.
C. Add it to issue log.
D. Implement agreed response.
E. Plan a work around.

Correct answer

C – Add it to issue log

Question 2

You are working in organization as risk manager, your project manager has asked should we move a head for the risk or not, the probability that risk will occur and have positive impact is $5000 is 60 % whereas negative impact is $6000, and probability is 40%. What would you recommend?

A. Go ahead its positive risk.
B. Plan for negative risk
C. You need more information.
D. Escalate to subject matter expert.

Correct answer

A – Go ahead its positive risk

Question 3

You have identified the risk. It is a negative risk, you decided to change the plan. What are strategies you have used?

A. Mitigate
B. Avoid
C. Transfer
D. Escalate

Correct answer
B – Avoid

Question 4

A project manager is preparing for a meeting to identify risk associated with the project. As a part of the preparation, the project manager is looking for a document that captures a comprehensive list of factors that could either benefit or constraints the project. Which of the following would help the project manager most?

A. Assumption log
B. Issue log
C. Risk register
D. Project charter

Correct answer

A – Assumption log

Question 5

During project execution, the project manager learns of a new government regulation that will impact her commercial building construction project. Specifically, regulatory compliance will now require the addition of a redundant fire suppression system. This risk has been identified during initial project and appropriate contingency serves were allocated. Which of the following project artifacts will be updated because of this regulatory change?

A. Cost baseline
B. Scope baseline
C. Risk register
D. Change management plan.
E. Activity list
F. Configuration management plan
G. Change log.

Correct answer – A, B, C, G

7. QUALITY

Quality Management

Quality has been defined in a number of different ways. When viewed from a consumer's perspective, it means meeting or exceeding customer expectations. The extent to which a product satisfies a set of inherited requirements or characteristics is referred to as quality. What you promise the buyer is quality. What the buyer pays for is quality. But what he purchases, you first concur with them. If you agree to give a product that will last for about five years, then the lifespan of your product should be five years. Most of the time, quantity and quality are co-related. Even though you promised high quality, it is probable that your product is not the most expensive one on the market. Whatever you and the customer agree upon must be provided; this becomes your standard of quality, which you must uphold. At the end of the day, it is possible that you spend more money than you had anticipated. Most of the time, we seek product requirement compliance. The aggregate standard has no variance, hence there is no need for more labor. Whatever standard of quality you adhere to, one thing is certain i.e., there must be no defects. Standards are a written model that has been accepted by a customer or an authority. Standards are not set by a government organization.

Following are a variety of quality standards:

1. ISO standard
2. ISO 9000 series
3. ISO health and safety standards
4. OSHA standards for health and safety
5. Double a triple a center for the aeronautics.

Regulations are requirements imposed by a governmental body. These requirements can establish product, process, or service characteristics, including applicable administrative provisions that have government mandated compliance.

Compliance is a type of audit that you must pass, or you risk failing.

Types of Compliance

- Quality compliance
- Health and safety compliance

Quality Management Plan

Quality management is the process of identifying and administering the activities necessary to achieve the organization's quality objectives. The Quality Management Plan, or QMP. Your quality management plan will outline the rules and regulations to which you will adhere. It outlines the work being done and the resources needed by the project management team. They will take the necessary actions to fulfil the goal or meet the quality-imposed requirement. Plans may be formal or casual in nature. It is customized in accordance with the demands of the company. We evaluate the quality plan and establish the benchmarks. We deliver the quality plan to the client when it has been accepted.

Quality Metrics

Key Performance Indicators (KPI) are developed to understand the overall health of an organization. They provide the fundamental element of balanced scorecards and dashboards, which are used to quickly show how well the organization is performing relative to the past, a target, or both. The choice of metric is important only as far as the metric is used to guide behavior or establish strategy. Once chosen, the metrics must be communicated to the members of the organization.

Benchmarking is a popular method for developing requirements and setting goals. In more conventional terms, benchmarking can be defined as measuring your performance against that of best-in class companies, determining how the best-in-class achieve those performance levels, and using the information as the basis for your own company's targets, strategies, and implementation. Benchmarking to the ISO quality standard is no longer required. The strategy you develop internally for your own organization is also acceptable. Benchmarking is based on learning from others, rather than developing new and improved approaches. However, if you are establishing a state of art project that has never been attempted before and no quality standards have been recognized earlier, we turn to consult the professionals for their expert opinion, and the SMEs will explain which standard to use and how to do so.

Quality Control

Quality control is the process used by operational personnel to ensure that their processes meet the product and service requirements (defined during the planning stage). It is based on the feedback loop and consists of the following steps:

- Evaluate actual operating performance
- Compare actual performance with goals.
- Act on the difference.

Cost of Quality

The fundamental principle of the cost of quality is that any cost that would not have been expended if quality were perfect is a cost of quality. This includes obvious costs such as scrap and rework, but it also includes many costs that are far less obvious, for instance the cost of reordering to replace defective material. These costs must be approved before they can be included in the cost management strategy, considering that the cost of quality is fully accounted for in the cost management strategy.

Quality costs are a measure of the costs specifically associated with the Achievement (Cost of Conformance) or Non-Achievement (Cost of Non-conformance) of product or service quality—including all product or service requirements established by the company and its contracts with customers and society. Cost of Quality helps define and measure where and what amount of an organization's resources are being used for prevention activities and maintaining product quality, as opposed to the costs resulting from internal and external failures.

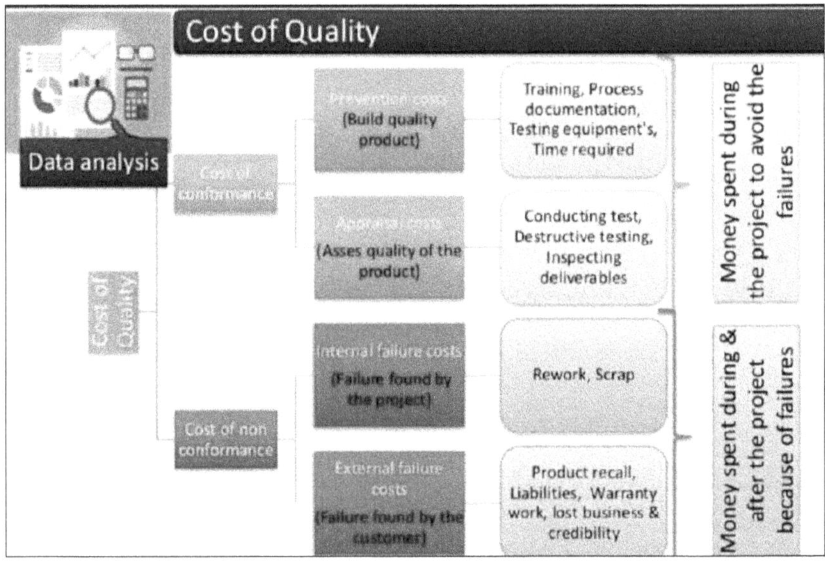

Cost of conformance <u>cost incurred to prevent failures;</u> (Manage Quality)

1. Non-destructive testing
2. Appraisals
3. Trainings
4. Checklist

Cost of non-conformance cost incurred because of failures due to poor quality; (Control Quality)

1. Rework -within the organization
2. Destructive testing
3. Warranty cost- the price of producing a product and sending it to the customer. The customer said that this product was incorrect and that it needed to be changed.

The quality management strategy has now been completed and is ready for submission to the organization for approval. As soon as the quality management plan has been approved by the organization, quality planning can be put into practice.

Quality Audit

An audit is a comparison of observed activities and/or results with documented requirements. The evidence provided from audits forms the basis of improvement in either the element audited, or in the requirements. Effective quality auditing can prevent problems by uncovering situations that, while still acceptable, are trending toward an eventual problem. The attention of management brought on by an unfavorable audit report can often prevent future noncompliance.

Quality Report

A project document that includes quality management issues, recommendations for corrective actions, and a summary of findings from quality control activities and may include recommendations for process, project, and product improvements.

Quality Management Tools

1) Checklist - A checklist is simple; we simply check each item off as we proceed.

2) Control chart - A Six Sigma control chart is a statistical tool used in the field of quality management to monitor and control a process over time. It is a graphical representation that displays data points plotted against predetermined control limits. The control chart helps identify any variations or trends in the process performance, allowing organizations to take corrective actions and maintain process stability. By using statistical analysis, the control chart helps determine if a process is within acceptable limits or if it requires adjustment or intervention to improve its performance and reduce defects.

I. Seven-point rule

Continuously having seven points outside the mean, either upwards or downwards, indicates an issue with your control chart or process.

II. Any point that goes out of the limit

Any sample that exceeds the threshold. For instance, a bottle should be one foot long, but it is 1.5 feet long, exceeding the allowed length, so we must stop. It should be about 10 inches, but it is only 5 inches, which is less than the maximum. Any point that is over the limit or beyond our ability to regulate indicates an issue with our process, and we must act. We must perform an RCA, or root cause analysis.

3) Root Cause Analysis RCA

The goal of a root cause analysis is to find the root of the issue. There are two ways to conduct a Root Cause Analysis.

I. **5 Why or 4W + H** - A simple, quick method for getting from symptoms to the root cause of a problem by repeatedly asking "why" logic chain.

II. **Fishbone diagram,** sometimes called an Ishikawa diagram/ Cause and Effect diagram, or a schematic of root causes. You construct a fishbone, set an issue on the fish's face, and analyze the causes and effects as shown in the figure below.

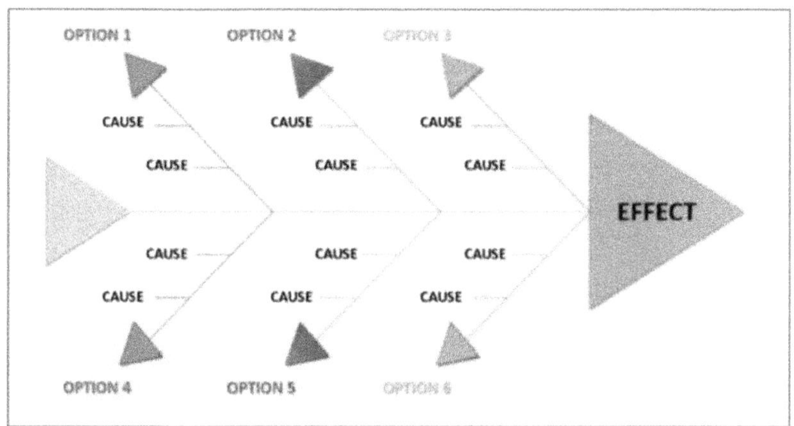

[Reference: Ft Maintenance Root Cause Analysis Diagram]

4) Sampling

Sampling technique is the process of selecting a representative subset of a larger population for inspection or testing. The purpose of sampling is to obtain information about the quality of the entire population by examining a smaller, more manageable sample.

Sampling can be used in various project management contexts, such as quality control and risk management. For example, in quality control, a project manager may use sampling to inspect a representative sample of products or materials to ensure that they meet the required quality standards. In risk management, a project manager may use sampling to identify potential risks by examining a representative sample of project data or information.

Types of Sampling

1- Attribute sampling

Zero attribute mean when anything is checked, it either passes or fails.

2- Variable sampling

Statistical sampling is also used by some organizations. What occurs during a statistical sample is we choose to examine one bottle after every 100 bottles i.e., by selecting a random sample.

Control Quality

The Control Quality process involves several activities, including inspecting and testing project deliverables, reviewing project documentation, and verifying that project work meets the required quality standards. The process also involves identifying and documenting any defects or errors found during the inspection and testing process and taking corrective action to address them.

1) Inspection

It is determining whether the quality standards are met or not. It is strange that the client is not here right now. You are internally determining whether the product satisfies the quality criteria. If it does not, you remedy it by doing something. Manage quality and control quality differ in that:

- Manage quality is preventive action.
- Control quality is a corrective action.

2) Check sheets

Check sheets are tally sheets that count the number of defects.

3) Histogram

A frequency distribution is a histogram. A straightforward graph to create a frequency distribution diagram of something distinct.

4) Pareto Principle (Rule of Vital Few and Trivial Many)

This principle is also referred to as the 80/20 rule: 80% of the trouble comes from 20% of the problems. Though named for turn-of-the-century economist Vilfredo Pareto, it was Dr. Juran who applied the idea to management. By identifying the most significant risks or quality issues, project managers can focus their efforts on addressing the most critical areas and improving project outcomes.

5) Flowchart

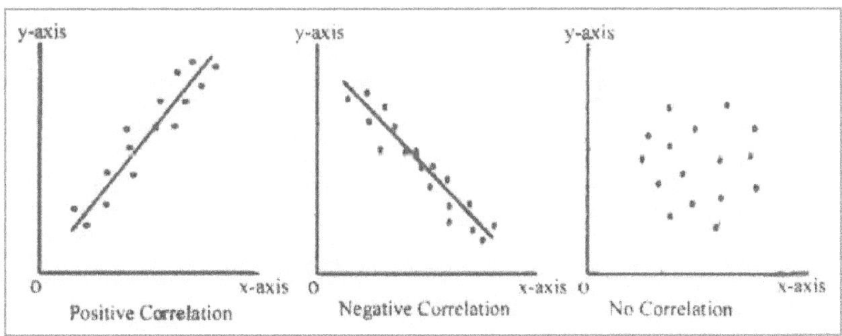

A flowchart depicts the steps in a process.

6) **Scatter Diagram**

It is a correlation diagram. When two variables are correlated, what will happen if we increase one together with the other variable is examined.

Positive correlation occurs when one variable increases while the other also increases.

- Negative correlation occurs when one variable increase while the other decreases.
- There is **no correlation**, or relationship, between the two variables.

7) **DOX - Design of X** refers to altering one design parameter while maintaining the status quo for all other parameters. We do it to optimize the design and select the best from the prototypes.

8) **Questionnaire & Surveys** – helps assess quality through a series of questions pertinent to a product, service, or performance.

9) **Definition of Done** - It is a checklist to ensure that the client has acceptance standards, and the quality is present.

10) **Brainstorming** – Brainstorming is a team-based strategy for quickly capturing diverse information, ideas, and perspectives.

11) **Affinity Diagram** – Refers to a tool for organizing ideas generated during a brainstorming session into groups by - similarity. It organizes ideas into categories so that they are easier to understand.

Pareto vs. Fishbone Diagram

It is important to note that the purpose of the Pareto chart is to prioritize, using the 20/80 principle to identify the vital few and focus on them.

The Fishbone diagram, also known as the Ishikawa diagram, Why-Why-Why diagram, or root cause analysis diagram, is used to delve deeper into a problem and understand the issues at hand, as well as how to overcome them.

In fact, the sequence for solving any quality problem is as follows:

- Step 1: Use a checklist to capture data.
- Step 2: Graph the data using a histogram.
- Step 3: Use Pareto charts to map the most important defects.
- Step 4: Use root cause analysis to identify the problem.
- Step 5: Solve the problem and repeat these steps as necessary to address any issues.

Journey of Deliverable

Following approval of the business case and benefit management plan, the project charter is created. Once the project charter is authorized, we then create a project management plan.

As soon as we have established a project management plan, we begin working on its subsidiary plans. This is the method through which the job is completed or delivered. Deliverables, or the actual work, is produced by us.

In a typical project scenario, a deliverable transition from a verified deliverable to an accepted deliverable through a two-step process: quality control and validation, followed by formal acceptance by the stakeholders.

Quality Control and Validation: Once a deliverable is completed, it undergoes a quality control process to ensure it meets the project's quality standards and requirements. This process may involve inspections, testing, or peer reviews. The project team checks the deliverable against the project's quality management plan and the agreed-upon acceptance criteria. If the deliverable meets these criteria, it is considered a **verified deliverable**. If it does not, the team must address any issues or defects and repeat the quality control process until the deliverable is verified.

Formal Acceptance by the Stakeholder: After a deliverable has been verified, it is presented to the client for their review and approval. The client evaluates the deliverable based on the acceptance criteria and their expectations. If they are satisfied with the deliverable, they provide formal acceptance, and the deliverable becomes an **accepted deliverable**. This acceptance is typically documented through a sign-off or approval process. If the client is not satisfied, they may request changes or revisions by submitting a formal change request, and the project team must address these concerns and resubmit the deliverable for acceptance.

In summary, a deliverable becomes an accepted deliverable by first being verified through quality control, and then receiving formal acceptance from the client. This process ensures that the deliverable meets the project's quality standards and satisfies client expectations.

PRACTICE EXAM QUESTIONS

Question 1

You are the project manager of a construction company, you have noticed that some of the team members are not working to agree standards, you want to check we are following the processes or not, what will you do?

A- An organizational audit
B- Senior customer review
C- A customer audit
D- A quality audit

Correct Answer
D – Quality audit

Question 2

Which of the following is not the goal of quality assurance?
A- Ensure appropriate quality standards have been set up for the project.
B- Verify the project results comply with the relevant quality standards.
C- Ensure continuous quality improvements.
D- Confirm that project quality activities confirm to quality policies and procedures.

Correct Answer
A-Ensure appropriate quality standards have been set up for the project.

Question 3

You are working in an operation organization and there have been reported a lot of errors in the past few months. You want to know to prioritize which issue you should focus on first, your goal is to target a big issue first, and then you will go for other issue. Which tool will help you in this process?

A- Matrix diagrams

B- Flow chart

C- SWOT Analysis

D- Pareto chart

Correct Answer

D – Pareto Chart

Question 4

You are making a quality management plan; this is a state of art project. You are not sure which standards you can use for this project and must compare the quality standards. What will you do?

A- Statistical sampling

B- Benchmarking

C- Run chart.

D- Expert judgment

Correct answer

D – Expert judgment

Question 5

The client has rejected the deliverable as you did root cause analysis you find that it does not meet quality standards as agreed with the client. Which procedure/ tool need improvement to avoid such issue in the future?

A- You need to manage quality better.

B- Use 6 sigma to manage quality.

C- Control quality needs improvement.

D- Benchmark the right standards.

Correct Answer

C – Control quality needs improvement.

8. PROCUREMENT

Procurement Management

Project procurement management is focused on planning for and making decisions about whether to procure goods and services needed on the project from external sources, which form of contact to choose, how to select sellers to deliver the work, and how to check that the work is being done in accordance with the agreed contracts.

The procurement effort on projects varies widely and depends on the type of project. Often the client organization will provide procurement services on less complex projects. In this case, the project team identifies the materials, equipment, and supplies needed by the project and provides product specifications and a detailed delivery schedule.

On larger, more complex projects, personnel are dedicated to procuring and managing the equipment, supplies, and materials needed by the project. Because of the temporary nature of projects, equipment, supplies, and materials are procured as part of the product of the project or for the execution of the project.

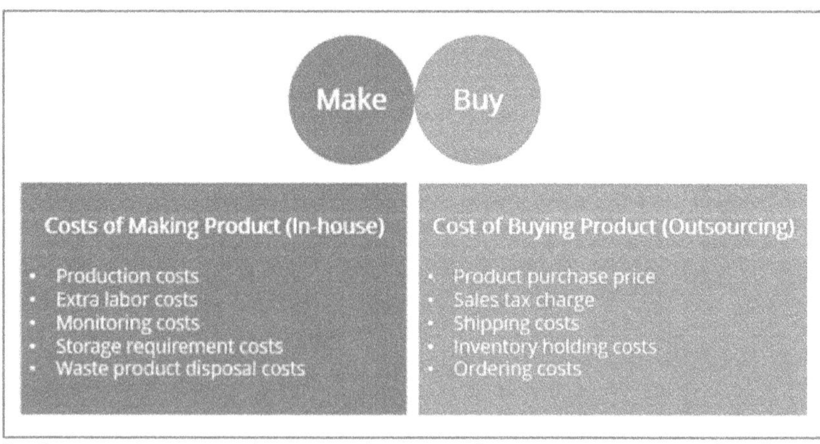

[Reference: Corporate Finance Institute – Make or Buy Decision Analysis]

Make or Buy?

The make-or-buy analysis is a comprehensive description of the decision-making process an organization goes through when deciding whether it should make the goods or services it requires itself or seek to acquire goods or services from external sources. There are a number of ways of making the decision and a number of factors to consider.

- What is the impact on cost, time, or quality?
- Is there an ongoing need for the specific skill set?
- How steep is the learning curve?
- Are required resources readily available within the organization?

What Are the Factors That Leads to Your Buying Decision?

Of the factors that can be considered when making a make-or-buy decision, the following are the most important:

- The organization's risk profile and risk tolerance
- Ownership of intellectual property
- Availability of suitable sellers
- Availability of internal resources capable of delivering a good or service
- Timeframes for delivery of a good or service
- Length of time the resource required for the good or service is needed on the project.
- Ability to support ongoing changes and technical support.

The make-or-buy process should follow established procedures that consider the relevant factors. We can even assign weights to various factors to enable you to score factors differently which answers the following 4W+1H of procurement.

- What to buy
- Where to buy- experience, qualified vendors,
- When to buy
- Why to buy
- How much

Source Selection Criteria refers to a set of attributes desired by the buyer which a seller is required to meet or exceed to be selected for a contract. Some of these are:

- Overall or life-cycle cost
- Understanding of need
- Technical capability
- Management approach
- Warranty
- Financial capacity
- Production capacity and interest
- Business size and type
- Past performance of sellers
- References
- Intellectual property rights

Single Source vs. Sole Source

Single source – Buyer selects a single company or seller to provide the product or service. Buyer can select other sellers, but preference is for a specific seller.

Sole source – Only one seller can provide the needed product or service. Has a monopoly in its market and tremendous leverage with most buyers.

Type of Contracts

Fixed Price Contract: Sellers under fixed-price contracts are legally obligated to complete such contracts, with possible financial damages if they do not. Under the fixed-price arrangement, buyers need to precisely specify the product or services being procured. Changes in scope may be accommodated, but with an increase in contract price.

I. **Firm Fixed Price (FFP)** The most used contract type is the FFP. It is favored by most buying organizations because the price for goods is set at the outset and not subject to change unless the scope of work changes. Any cost increase due to adverse performance is the responsibility of the seller, who is obligated to complete the effort. Under the FFP contract, the buyer should precisely specify the product or services to be procured and any changes to the procurement specification can increase the costs to the buyer.

II. **Fixed Price Incentive Fee (FPIF)** This fixed-price arrangement gives the buyer and seller some flexibility in that it allows for deviation from performance, with financial incentives tied to achieving agreed upon metrics. Typically, such financial incentives are related to cost, schedule, or technical performance of the seller. Performance targets are established at the outset, and the final contract price is determined after completion of all work based on the seller's performance. Under FPIF contracts, a price ceiling is set, and all costs above the price ceiling are the responsibility of the seller, who is obligated to complete the work.

III. **Fixed Price Economic Price Adjustment (FP-EPA)** - This contract type is used whenever the seller's performance period spans a considerable period of years, as is desired with many long-term relationships. It is a fixed-price contract but with a special provision allowing for pre-defined final adjustments to the contract price due to changed conditions, such as inflation changes, or cost increases (or decreases) for specific commodities. The FP-EPA contract is intended to protect both buyer and seller from external conditions beyond their control.

Cost Reimbursable Contract: This category of contract involves payments (cost reimbursements) to the seller for all legitimate actual costs incurred for completed work, plus a fee representing seller profit. A cost-reimbursable contract provides the project flexibility to redirect a seller whenever the scope of work cannot be precisely defined at the start and needs to be altered, or when high risks may exist in the effort.

I. **Cost Plus Fixed Fee Contracts (CPFF)** The seller is reimbursed for all allowable costs for performing the contract work and receives a fixed-fee payment calculated as a percentage of the initial estimated project costs. A fee is paid only for completed work and does not change due to seller performance. Fee amounts do not change unless the project scope changes.

II. **Cost Plus Incentive Fee Contracts (CPIF)** The seller is reimbursed for all allowable costs for performing the contract work and receives a predetermined incentive fee based upon achieving certain performance objectives as set forth in the contract.

III. **Cost Plus Award Fee Contracts (CPAF)** The seller is reimbursed for all legitimate costs, but most of the fee is earned only based on the satisfaction of certain broad subjective performance criteria defined and incorporated into the contract.

Time and Material Contracts (T&M).

Time and material contracts are a hybrid type of contractual arrangement that contain aspects of both cost-reimbursable and fixed-price contracts. They are often used for staff augmentation, acquisition of experts, and any outside support when a precise statement of work cannot be quickly prescribed. These types of contracts resemble cost-reimbursable contracts in that they can be left open ended and may be subject to a cost increase for the buyer. The full value of the agreement and the exact quantity of items to be delivered may not be defined by the buyer at the time of the contract award. Thus, T&M contracts can increase in contract value as if they were cost reimbursable contracts. Many organizations require not-to-exceed values and time limits placed in all T&M contracts to prevent unlimited cost growth.

Conversely, T&M contracts can also resemble fixed unit price arrangements when certain parameters are specified in the contract. Unit labor or material rates can be preset by the buyer and seller, including seller profit, when both parties agree on the values for specific resource categories, such as senior engineers at specified rates per hour, or categories of materials at specified rates per unit.

Independent Estimate for the Consultant

For many procurement items, the procuring organization may elect to either prepare its own independent estimate or have an estimate of costs prepared by an outside professional estimator, to serve as a benchmark on proposed responses.

Procurement Management Plan is based on the project scope, budget, and schedule and ensures that the resources you need throughout the project are available at the right time so that you can meet the project requirements,

- It outlines the procurement process as a whole.
- When we can procure
- How the structure will perform.

PROCUREMENT STATEMENT OF WORK

The statement of work (SOW) for each procurement is developed from the project scope baseline and defines only that portion of the project scope that is to be included within the related contract. The procurement SOW describes the procurement item in sufficient detail to allow prospective sellers to determine if they are capable of providing the products, services, or results. Sufficient detail can vary based on the nature of the item, the needs of the buyer, or the expected contract form. Information included in a SOW can include specifications, quantity desired, quality levels, performance data, period of performance, work location, and other requirements.

After writing the procurement statement of work, we publish it as an advertisement and request bids from vendors. There is an advertisement, and then there is a bid process. A bidder conference is held when we receive multiple number of bids.

Bidder conference - These are meetings with prospective sellers prior to the preparation of a bid or proposal to ensure all prospective vendors have a clear and common understanding of the procurement. Also known as contractor conferences, vendor conferences, or pre-bid conferences. One of the goals of the builder conference is to gather all the sellers in one location. Buyer explains the requirements, proposed terms, and conditions and clarifies the vendors' queries. Consequently, the vendors offer their prices or quotations when the bidder conference is over.

Request for Information (RFI) – A type of procurement document whereby the buyer requests a potential seller to provide various pieces of information related to a product, service, or seller.

Request for Quotation (RFQ) – A type of procurement document used to request price quotations from prospective sellers of common or standard products or services.

Request for Proposal (RFP) – The RFP provides an overview of the project to give the bidding companies a clear description of what is needed and how they can help accomplish those goals. It will explain the process and contract terms to guide bidders. Most organizations conduct business using RFPs, and governments always conduct their business this way.

PRO TIP: The project manager does not engage in any type of discussion involving money, he or she is there to discuss about the scope and quality to make sure the organization is receiving the appropriate stuff. The procurement manager is responsible for handling the monetary aspect of procurement.

Procurement Contract includes terms and conditions and may incorporate other items that the buyer specifies as to what the seller is to perform or provide. It is the project management team's responsibility to make certain that all procurements meet the specific needs of the project while adhering to organizational procurement policies. Depending upon the application area, a contract can also be called an agreement, an understanding, a subcontract, or a purchase order. Most organizations document policies and procedures specifically defining the procurement rules and specifying who has authority to sign and administer such agreements on behalf of the organization.

Manage Procurement or Conduct Procurement

Manage procurement, also known as a conduct procurement, is the process where you receive bidder confidence, review all the bids, and sign the contract.

Audit

It is evaluating the process's efficiency. How well your procedure works. If you want to audit the process, the contract must specifically state that you are permitted to do so. Otherwise, you cannot conduct the organization's audit. The fact that you wish to conduct an audit of that organization must be highlighted. That must be specified in that specific contract.

Inspection

Inspection entails examining the deliverables and confirming them in accordance with your contract. If you both concurred on the deliverable, the procurement was successful, and the paperwork are closed after payment. However, a dispute arises if you disagree with the deliverable. Now to resolve the dispute, we carry out an inspection or walkthrough and seal the deal.

CONTRACT CANCELLATION

1. Cancellation for Convenience

- Buyer pays for all work up to point of cancellation, regardless of whether accepted or not.
- Buyer cancels

2. Cancellation for Cause

- Default by either party
- Default by seller – buyer pays only for accepted work.
- May result in legal action.

3. Alternate Dispute Resolution – ADR

- **Mediator:** When everything else fails, you turn to a mediator who acts as a neutral third party to try to mediate a resolution between the parties.

- **Go to the court:** Settlement through negotiation is preferred. You should avoid going to court since it will be expensive and time-consuming.

Control Procurements Process

The process of managing procurement relationships, monitoring contract performance, making changes and as appropriate, and closing out contracts.

Close Procurement is also known as the contract closure, it supports the close project or close phase processes. Procurement is said to be closed when the contract deadline is reached and ends, or when the contract is terminated. A project can have a single procurement contract or multiple contracts.

The close procurement process will happen only once per procurement contract. However, if the project has multiple procurement contracts, the close procurement process will be performed multiple times because there are many contracts.

Close Project Process

The Close project or phase is the process of finalizing all activities across all the project management process groups to formally complete the project or phase. This definition shows that the close project or close phase process is performed when the project or phase is finally completed, and deliverables are accepted.

To complete the close project or close phase process, the close procurement process must have been completed; otherwise, the former cannot happen—however, it is different for the close procurement process where the project does not have to be finished to complete the close procurement process.

Close Procurements Vs. Close Project

One of the keyways to distinguish this process from the Close Procurements process is that the Close Project or Phase process is focused not only on contractual closure but on all the aspects of administrative closure as well. Being an integrated process, it considers how contractual closure processes as part of the Close

Procurements process may impact other areas of the project, and it also goes through the defined and approved closure process the organization has as part of its organizational process assets.

- The close procurement process must happen before the close project or close phase process.
- The close procurement process may occur many times during the project's life cycle, but the close project process will be performed only once at the end of the project.
- In the close project or close phase processes, the client accepts the deliverables.

- The close procurement process may or may not occur, but every project must pass through the close project process even if it is terminated.

- In close procurement, you close your deal with your contractor, and in the close project process your client closes the deal with you.

PRACTICE EXAM QUESTIONS

Question 1

You are witnessing a procurement negation of a project that you all manage. The negotiations are being carried out by your company's procurement manager and team. You notice the seller trying to overprice by including numerous hidden charges. Which of the following best describes an objective of contract negotiations?

A. Arriving at a reasonable and mutually acceptable price
B. Undercutting seller prices
C. Creation of the procurement management plan
D. Identification of all project risks and risk to the seller

Correct answer

A – Arriving at a reasonable and mutually acceptable price

Question 2

As the project manager for a subcontractor responsible for the designs and installation of an HVAC in a large regional hospital, you lead weekly walk-throughs of the work program with the buyer and more contractor. What control procurement tool and technique are you using to ensure all parties have a mutual understanding of the work in progress?

A. Audit
B. Inspection
C. Data analysis
D. Claims administration.

Correct answer

B – Inspection

Question 3

You are project manager of a network replacement project for 40 floor office building. You plan to hire a contractor to replace the cables. The work must be completed in such a way to have minimum to zero disruption to the organization during business hours. Due to the complexity and risk inherent in this constraint, you believe it necessary that a firm with a significant experience and a track record of success he contracted. You contracted the procurement department to develop a list of firms that have the capability to do the work. What should the procurement do next?

A. Prepare the list of qualified sellers.
B. Develop the evaluation criteria.
C. Negotiate a contract with an experienced firm.
D. Prepare a solidification package to be sent out to prospective sells.

Correct answer

A – Prepare the list of qualified sellers

Question 4

A service provider contests the payment your company has made, stating that he should be paid 2500 dollar more than what he has currently received for the number of hours worked. Negotiations with the service provider has failed. What should be the next best thing to do?

A. Do nothing.
B. Negotiate once again but this time involve yourself and the CEO of your company.
C. Initiate the alternative dispute resolution mechanism.
D. Take the service provider to court.

Correct Answer

C – Initiate the alternative dispute resolution mechanism

Question 5

What type of contact is most used when the product specifications are very detailed, well defined, and not likely to change?

A. Time lapsed.
B. Cost reimbursable.
C. Fixed price or lump sum
D. Time and material

Correct answer

C – Fixed price or lump sum

9. SCOPE

Scope Management

Scope in project management refers to the specific boundaries and deliverables of a project. A project's scope is usually established in a project scope statement, which outlines the project's goals, deliverables, and prerequisites. The scope statement also incorporates any limitations or assumptions that may affect the project's success. The project's scope is crucial since it guarantees that the project remains on course and that all stakeholders have a comprehensive understanding of what is anticipated.

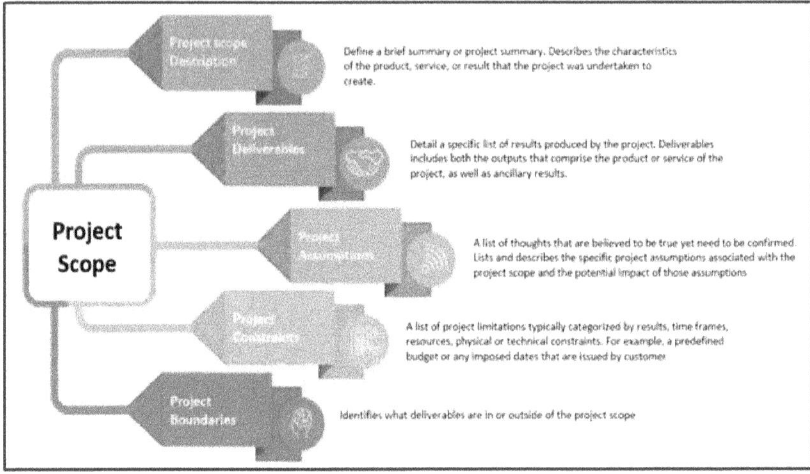

[Reference: Power Slides Project Scope Template]

In the project context, the term scope can refer to:

1. Product Scope
2. Project Scope

Product Scope The agreed-upon conditions or capabilities of a product, service, or outcome that the project is designed to satisfy. The life cycle of a product begins with a requirement analysis, followed by the creation of a business case, a benefits management plan, a project charter, the actual execution of the project, the closing of the project, its operation, and finally its termination.

Project Scope The actions, processes, or other conditions the project needs to meet e.g., milestone dates, contractual obligations, constraints, etc. The project charter is where the pmp's scope begins. The product life cycle begins with the creation of the project charter and ends when the project is completed. The project is designed with the ability to go from conception to operation. A project is anything that offers value and initiates your project; therefore, both are quite significant. A product is a broader thing, and a project is a smaller or a subset of it.

Types Of Requirements

Business: Higher-level needs of the organization e.g., business issues or opportunities, and reasons why a project has been undertaken.

Stakeholder: Stakeholder or stakeholder group needs. Reporting requirements.

Transition and Readiness: Temporary capabilities, e.g., data conversion and training requirements needed to transition from the current as-is state to the desired future state.

Quality: Condition or criteria needed to validate the successful completion of a project deliverable or fulfilment of other project requirements e.g., tests, certifications, validations.

Project Actions, processes, or other conditions the project needs to meet e.g., milestone dates, contractual obligations, and constraints.

Scope of Project Management Plan

The project life cycle is more the focus of the project management plan. However, when we gather all the project's needs for every aspect of the product and project. What are we to do? Because the project is a subset of the product, which will have all the criteria, we gather the requirements for the product. It will have the specifications for a project and a finished result. Therefore, everything is immediately covered when you fulfill that criterion. Therefore, gathering the requirements in the project management plan is one of the most crucial things we need to perform in this situation.

DEFINE SCOPE: TOOLS AND TECHNIQUES

- **Expert Opinion**

We turn to the subject-matter expert and enquire about the project's needs that must be met.

- **Focus Group**

We can assemble 8 to 12 subject matter specialists. Focus on a subject, hence the name "focus group." Eight to twelve subject-matter specialists are present. The facilitator directs the session, and we brainstorm together.

- **Brainstorming**

A method for generating ideas is brainstorming. Since brainstorming generates random ideas, it is possible to classify them once they have been created.

- **Mind Mapping**

An information flow chart where any type of structure can be created.

- **Affinity Diagram**

Simply classifying it by names or in a different method based on sizes.

- **Facilitated workshop**

We can do a workshop for those who are older than 8 to 12 people. It follows the same format as brainstorming; ideas are generated, categorized, and occasionally voted on during that workshop to determine which are more crucial.

- **Documents**

We analyze our comprehensive project charter, which comprises a vast array of documents, to identify and understand the high-level requirements. Additionally, we thoroughly evaluate the provided lesson plans and the business case benefit management strategy within this section. Our objective is to ascertain the specific requirements outlined in the document and explore their potential applications. We employ various classification methods to categorize these demands and gain insights into their nature.

- **Prototype**

The prototype is something we create and present to the client.

- **Storyboarding/ Story map**

Agile primarily employs the story mapping to create a **minimal viable produc**t which meets the minimum requirements and is utilized for the specific marketing objective.

- **Value Stream Map**

We can employ a value stream map in lean. It consists of maps that show which project tasks provide value and which do not. We classify them. Learn more about it is the goal. Only get the task's value by removing the non-valued task from the object.

- **Context Diagram**

It resembles a graphic that depicts the entire environment and how each object interacts with the others.

Requirement Traceability Matrix (RTM)

A requirements traceability matrix (RTM) is **a tool that helps identify and maintain the status of the project's requirements and deliverables**. It does so by establishing a thread for each component.

- Who gathered the necessary data?
- What was the prerequisite?
- Who enquired about the prerequisite?
- What specifically was required?
- What was the requirement's success criterion or KPI?
- How far along is the requirement?
- How the prerequisite will be met?
- What will the requirement's priority be?

The requirement traceability matrix eliminates every single requirement detail. We put everything into the required traceability matrix after collecting it.

The significance of the requirement traceability matrix is that everything will be included in your project, and as time goes on, you may update it as needed. The references will be consistent and unique throughout the entire project. It will apply to both the project and the finished result.

Requirement Documentation

Requirements documentation describes how individual requirements meet the business need for the project. Requirements may start out at a high level and become progressively more detailed as more about the requirements is known. It merely divides the needs into various categories including business requirements, stakeholder requirements, solution requirements, project requirements, transition requirements, and other factors as well as functional requirements also called functional requirements. It organizes the specifications for projects and goods.

- **Functional Requirements**

Describes the behaviors of the product e.g., actions, processes, data, and interactions that the product should execute.

- **Non-Functional Requirements**

Describes environmental conditions or qualities required for the product to be effective. The requirements are organized according to the necessary supporting paperwork and compiles them all into metrics for requirement traceability. Now, in accordance with the requirement management plan, we have collected the requirements and added them to the necessary documentation and requirement traceability metrics using a variety of tools and methodologies. Since we are more interested in the project requirement, the next step is to **filter out the requirements** and separate the product requirements from the project requirements.

Project Scope Statement

All the criteria from the requirement traceability matrix are put through a filter, and if they pass, they become part of the project's requirements. We then record these criteria in a document called the project scope statement. **The project scope statement describes the project scope and its major deliverables, assumptions, and constraints.** Let us say that a client requires a 2000 square-foot house with four rooms, four air-conditioners, 300 down-lighters, and contemporary interiors delivered within six months, this information will be specified in the project scope statement and the project will be accepted based on this record.

Acceptance Criteria refers to the predefined requirements that must be met, taking all possible scenarios into account, to consider a user story to be finished. In other words, they specify the conditions under which a user story can be said to be 'done.' When all the criteria are met, the team can set the task aside and move on to the next story.

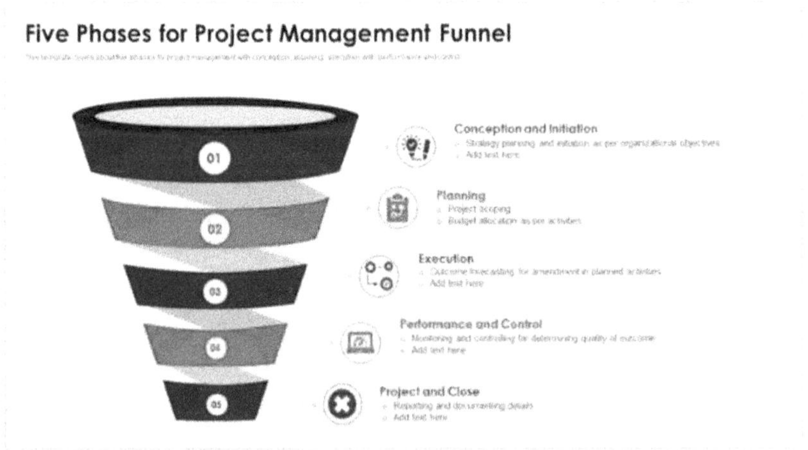

[Reference: Slide Team Five Phases of Project Management Funnel]

The scope management strategy establishes the project requirement and thus consists of both the requirement management plan and the scope management plan.

Requirements Management Plan

A requirement management strategy is in place. It will explain how to gather the necessary information. How can the necessary information be gathered? We employ a wide range of tools and techniques to gather the requirements.

Work Breakdown Structure

A WBS is a hierarchical **decomposition** of the total scope of work to be carried out by the project team to accomplish the project objectives and create the required deliverables.

For instance, let us consider that Burj Khalifa is the goal for all our deliverables. What will be the WBS?

- Civil work
- Electrical work
- Mechanical work
- Plumbing work
- IIVAC

We further deconstruct the tasks and divide them into small manageable parts, allotting the smallest part a certain reference number such as 1.1, we additionally breakdown the structure and establish a reference code 1.1.1, and keep on dividing till we reach the last bit of task. These numbers are referred as **Code of Account.** Each number indicates the work we will perform in sequence and the methods used to complete. Since the code numbers are difficult to comprehend, we create a WBS dictionary for reference.

ELEMENTS OF WORK BREAKDOWN STRUCTURE

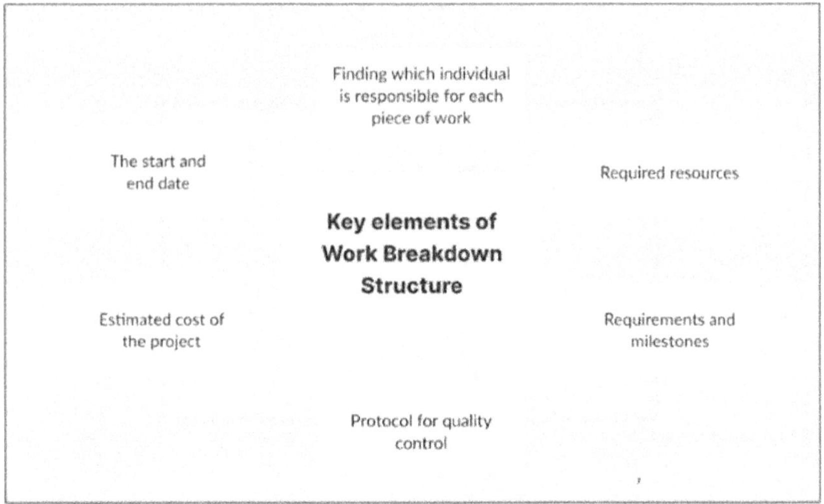

[Reference: Gantt Pro Blog WBS] https://blog.ganttpro.com/en/how-to-create-a-work-breakdown-structure-wbs-with-project-planning-templates/]

WBS Dictionary

Each dependency will be explained in detail for every item in the WBS lexicon. What does this account code mean?

Control Account

A control account is a management control point where scope, budget, actual cost, and schedule are integrated and compared to the earned value for performance measurement.

Planning Package

Every company has a unique WBS structure, and between the control account and the work package, there is a level where the planning team divides the work in accordance with them. This level is known as the planning package.

Work Package

A work package is the lowest level of the WBS hierarchy. The work package should involve an effort of 8 to 80 hours. To ensure that the effort is between 8 and 80 hours, you should break the WBS down into smaller components.

Scope Baseline

Scope Baseline = Project Scope Statement + Work Breakdown Structure + WBS Dictionary

We obtain sponsorship or **the change control board**'s approval. Once it has been accepted, nothing can be changed or added, and the client will only review the baseline scope items because the core baseline was decided upon by the client rather than the sponsor.

They will evaluate our work using this scope baseline to see whether it meets their needs or not, and they will either accept it or reject it. The most crucial document is the scope baseline, where every requirement must be included.

If the client has any requests, they must submit a modification request. The change request is then forwarded to the change control board for approval, and if granted, the scope baseline is updated. It is important to note that a baseline can only be changed through formal change control procedures. The baseline serves as a basis for comparison while performing Validate Scope and Control Scope.

Scope Creep occurs when a client continuously adds scope without submitting a change request.

Gold Plating is the process of enhancing a product with an additional feature.

Validate scope is the process via which the client approves or disapproves the deliverable.

How The Deliverable Goes to The Client?

The delivery of the final product or service to the client may involve a formal acceptance process, where the client reviews the deliverables to ensure that they meet their requirements. The quality team checks the deliverable to see if it complies with the quality management plan as part of quality control, as stated in the quality management plan. If the deliverables meet the requirements of the quality management plan, they are deemed validated deliverables.

Verified Deliverables

A verified deliverable is a completed project deliverable that has been checked and confirmed for correctness through the Control Quality process. Once the deliverable has been verified, it can be used in the Validate Scope process where it becomes an accepted deliverable.

Accepted Deliverables

- In accordance with the scope baseline, and if the customer deems the delivered product to be satisfactory, we receive a validated deliverable, sometimes referred to as an acceptable deliverable.
- If it does not meet the criteria, we receive a change request such as, a request for corrective action, a request for preventive action, or a request for faulty work (depending on the requirement)
- Finally, an accepted deliverable is used to close the project or phase.

Questionnaires and Survey- used especially when we are attempting to gather the requirements for a sizable population.

Benchmarking – used to determine the necessity of conformity, we utilize benchmark for comparison to what other people are doing to set a standard.

Interviews – are conducted when seeking to obtain confidential information.

PRACTICE EXAM QUESTIONS

Question 1

A client while inspecting the deliverable and has rejected it, will you check to make sure the deliverable was according to the requirement or not?

A. Project scope statement
B. Quality reports
C. Scope baseline
D. Scope management plan

Correct answer

C – Scope Baseline

Question 2

The project manager has developed a strong relationship with the customer. During a recent discussion, the customer requests a small change in the project scope. How should the project manager have responded to the request?

A. Refuse and explain that no changes can be made after the scope baseline is established.
B. Confirm that the changes will be placed in the backlog.
C. Ask the customer to provide the requested change in writing so that its impact can be reviewed.
D. Instruct the customer to request the change from the sponsor.

Correct Answer

C – Ask the customer to provide the requested change in writing so that its impact can be reviewed.

Question 3

You are collecting the requirement, you want to use the tool that will link the requirement with all the affected environments, which tool will you use?

A. Expert Judgment
B. Context diagram
C. Value stream mapping
D. Focus group.

Correct Answer

B – Context Diagram

Question 4

In which process client verify the deliverables

A. Control quality
B. Validate scope.
C. Create WBS
D. Monitor Scope

Correct Answer

B – Validate scope.

Question 5

Despite multiple requests, the project manager has been unable to organize a facilitated session in which all key stakeholders will provide key requirements. What approach should the project manager follow to obtain the requirements needed?

A. Submit a questionnaire to key stakeholders.
B. Schedule individual interviews with key stakeholders
C. Have the team define the key requirements.
D. Ask the sponsor to end the meeting.

Correct Answer

B – Schedule individual interviews with key stakeholders

10. SCHEDULE

Schedule Management

Schedules are a fundamental element of project management. It refers to a timeline or plan that outlines the tasks, activities, and milestones required to complete a project. The schedule typically includes start and end dates for each task, as well as dependencies between tasks and the resources required to complete them. The schedule is an essential component of project management, as it helps to ensure that the project is completed on time and within budget.

The schedule is typically created during the planning phase of a project and is continuously updated throughout the project's lifecycle. It is used to track progress, identify potential delays or issues, and adjust the project plan as needed. The schedule is also used to communicate project timelines and milestones to stakeholders, including the project team, clients, and other interested parties.

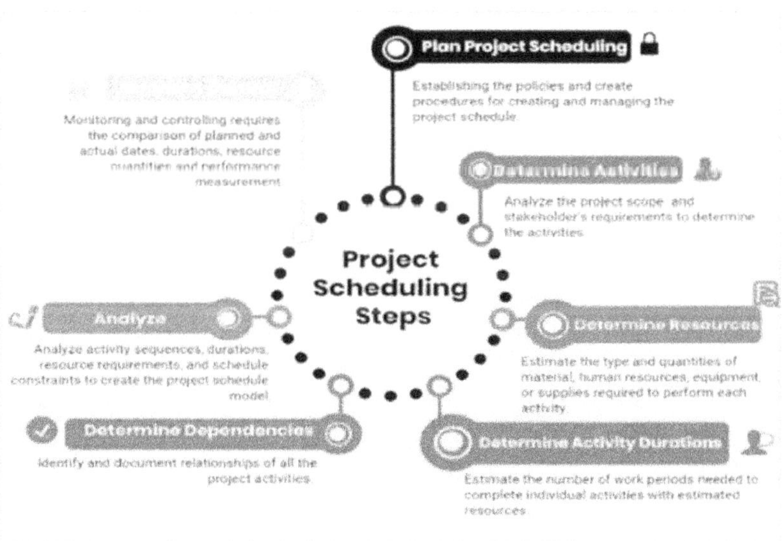

[Reference: Project Cubicle Project Scheduling Steps]

The schedule management strategy will specify which approach should be used and what software should be used. In Agile approach, schedules can be divided in the following types.

1) **Iterative Scheduling with a Backlog** – uses progressive elaboration (rolling wave) to schedule activities.

2) **Pull Based or On Demand System** - Based on Kanban and Lean Methodologies

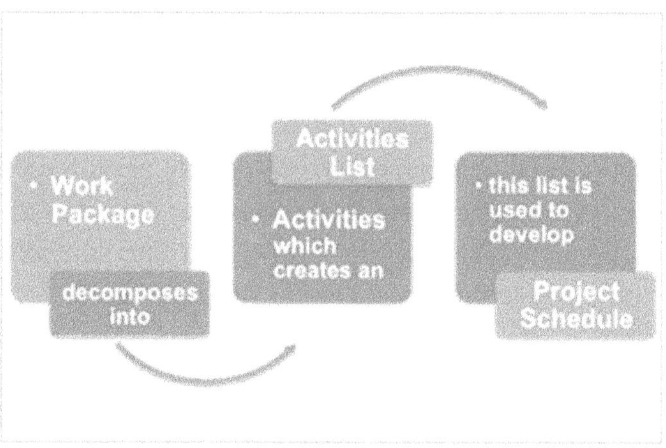

The working software can vary depending on the organizations for which you are working as each organization have different policies. So, let us start with the software. When you create a schedule management plan, the tolerance of that historical data will be specified. Then, you transmit your schedule management plan to the sponsor or the change control board for approval. We can move forward once your schedule management plan has been approved.

- Consists of start and finish activities
- Uses specific dates and in a certain sequence.
- Sets dates for project milestones.
- Coordinates activities to ensure on time project completion.

- Tracks schedule performance and provides visibility of project status to upper management and project stakeholders.

Develop A Schedule Management Plan

To develop an effective schedule management plan, we review the following components:

- Project management plan (for information to develop the schedule)
- Project charter (for a summary, high-level milestone schedule)
- EEFs
- OPAs
- Use tools and techniques such as expert judgment and historical information.
- Use meetings to develop the schedule management plan.

WORK BREAKDOWN STRUCTURE (WBS)

A work breakdown structure (WBS) is a scheduling tool that takes a step-by-step approach to complete large projects by breaking down the project into smaller components.

Work Package

A work package is the lowest level of the WBS. The work package will be further broken down into three parts.

- **Activity list**

An **activity** is a component of a decomposed work package. It depends on how many of those activities you define.

- **Activity attributes**

It contains all the information about such activities, including their dependencies, relationships, and duration.

Milestone List

A milestone list identifies all project milestones and indicates whether the milestone is mandatory based on historical information. Milestones have zero duration because they represent a significant point or event.

Gantt Chart

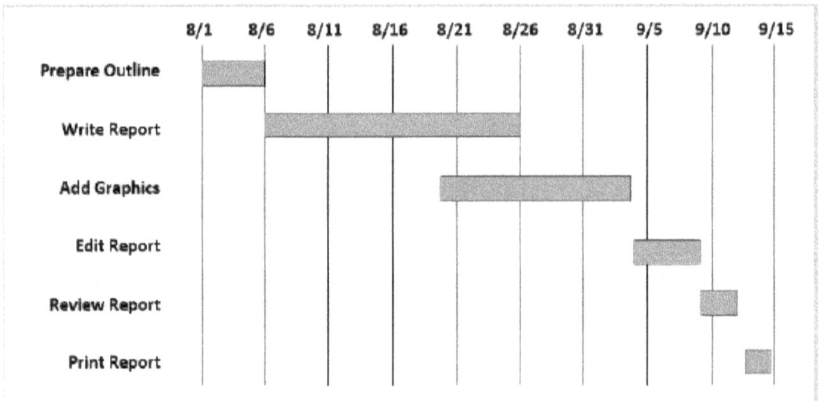

A Gantt chart shows the tasks in a sequential order and display task dependencies (i.e., how one task relates to another). It Identifies task relationships and decide on the completion date sequence for each task, showing the expected time duration of the whole project and the sub tasks.

Activity Dependency

Activity dependency indicates whether the start of an activity is contingent on an event or input from outside the activity. Activity dependencies determine the precedence relationships. There are four different kinds of precedence relationships.

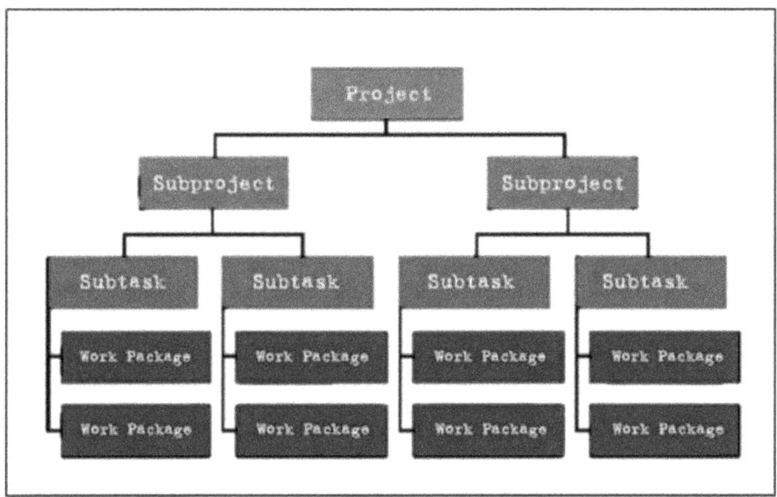

[Reference: T2 Informatik Work Breakdown Structure]

1. **Finish to Start activity**

- **Predecessor**
  The term "predecessor" refers to an earlier activity.
- **Successor**
  The activity that follows it is referred to as the successor.

2. **Start to Start relationship**
   Both activities beginning simultaneously

3. **Finish to finish relationship**
   You have no idea when such activities began, but we do since they conclude at the same time that a relationship does, finish to finish.

4. **Start to finish relationship**
   The predecessor action must begin for the successor activity to end. When there is a precise overlap between two activities, this activity is utilized.

Activity Dependencies are categorized as follows:

Any dependencies within the company are referred to as **Internal Dependencies**

Any dependencies outside the organization are called **External Dependencies**.

1- Mandatory Dependencies

Hard logic is another name for it. You must obtain a permission before beginning any work, both internal and external. They are both required dependencies.

2- Discretionary Dependencies

It is often referred to as soft logic preferred practices. There are solid practices you can use right now, so you can choose whatever ones you want to follow without being restricted in how you do something.

Project Estimates

A project estimate gives us a general idea of how much time, effort, and money it will take to get the job done. That makes it easier to build a feasible project budget and plan so you can set your team and organization up for success. There are numerous methods to estimate the project schedule.

1. Analogous Estimation

Analogous means same. Let us imagine that it took you six months to build a 200 square foot house. Now you need to build another house with the same size and layout. Since the parameters are same, i.e., size and layout, to the previously built house, we estimate the schedule for this project using analogous estimation.

2. Parametric Estimation

What if the dimension is altered? If it is doubled to 400 square feet, for example, the time will double; if it is cut in half to 100 square feet, the time will be cut in half. This statistical relationship is known as parametric estimation.

3. Three-point Estimation

In a three-point estimation, numerous points are used instead of a single point.

- **Optimistic- Best Case Scenario**
  Assuming everything goes as planned
- **Pessimistic - Worst Case Scenario**
  If all things work against you.
- **Most Likely**
  How long would it typically take?

Formulas to calculate the Estimated Schedule

- **Triangular distribution**
  Triangular Distribution=Optimistic + pessimistic + most likely/ 3
- **Beta distribution/ program evaluation and review technique**
  Beta Distribution= Optimistic + four most likely + pessimistic/ 6

4. Bottom-Up Estimation

Bottom-Up estimation involves breaking down the project into smaller, more manageable tasks and estimating the resources needed for each task individually. These individual task estimates are then aggregated to determine the overall project estimate.

Activity Node or Precedence Diagramming Method

Activity node or Precedence Diagramming Method (PDM) is a project management technique that uses nodes and arrows to represent project activities and their dependencies.

It helps project managers to identify critical paths and potential delays, allowing them to focus their efforts on completing activities on time and within budget. PDM is a valuable tool for creating a clear project schedule and managing potential issues.

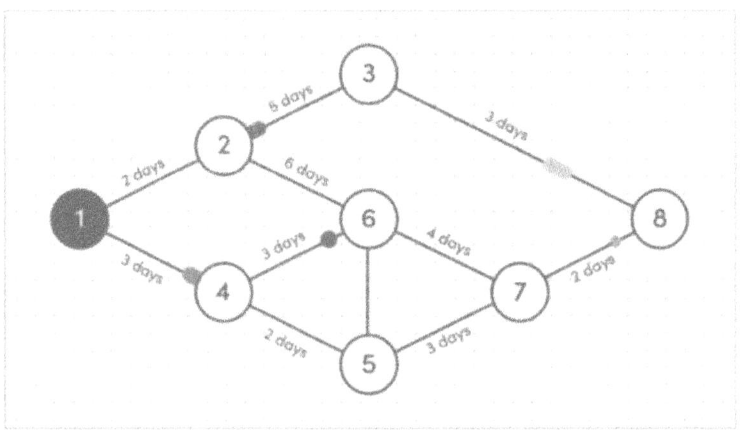

[Reference: Monday.com Blog Network]

- **Project Schedule Network Diagram**

A project schedule network diagram is a graphical representation of the logical relationships between the activities or tasks in a project. It visually depicts the sequence and dependencies of these activities, allowing project managers to understand the flow and interdependencies of the project schedule.

- **Critical Path**

The critical path is the project's longest route. It estimates the minimum project duration and determines the amount of schedule flexibility on the logical network paths within the schedule model. If any activity on critical path is delayed, the overall project duration would be delayed.

Float is the amount of time an activity can be delayed from its early start date without delaying the project finish date or consecutive activities.

Total float is the amount of time that a schedule activity can be delayed or extended from its early start date without delaying the project finish date or violating a schedule constraint.

Free float is the amount of time that a scheduled activity can be delayed without delaying the early start date of any successor or violating a schedule constraint.

Schedule Baseline

The schedule baseline is the planned schedule of the project after its approval by the relevant stakeholders. In project management, it is typically the output of the schedule development process and becomes a component of the project management plan.

The schedule baseline is used to measure and monitor the performance of a project: the delivered work at a point in time or over a period is compared against the baselined planned work at that time.

Schedule Compression Techniques

1- **Crashing**

We increase physical resources when we crash. It shortens the time, but the cost goes up as a drawback. If price is not a concern, we always do crashing.

2- **Fast tracking**

When you want to move quickly through a list of tasks, you make them parallel. The risk is decreased while parallelizing series action. If crashing is a possibility, we do not want to use fast tracking.

Resource Optimization Techniques

- **Resource Leveling**

When we level up our resources, we assess our available options and adjust our plan accordingly. There is a possibility that the timetable will raise the baseline.

- **Resource Smoothing**

Resource smoothing is just scheduling with a restriction. The schedule's rigidity is the restriction. You are unable to expand your schedule. Take any action you like during the interim.

PRACTICE EXAM QUESTIONS

Question 1

Midway into project execution, you have been asked to shorten your project duration by three weeks to meet a new deadline but deliver all originally planned functionality. Additional resources are available, and the cost is not as great concern as schedule. What should you do?

A- Crash activities on the critical path

B- Remove external dependencies.

C- Reduce scope project.

D- Level resources

Correct Answer

A – Crash activities on the critical path

Question 2

A project team has just completed estimates for both the activity durations and the activity resources for the project you are managing. Tomorrow morning, you need to present a preliminary schedule to key the stakeholders. What is your best course of action?

A- Pre- assign the resources required for the project.

B- Apply resource optimization technique.

C- Present the project schedule network diagram.

D- Develop the schedule management plan.

Correct Answer

A – Present the project schedule network diagram.

Question 3

Your sponsor has refused to increase the schedule. You are having problems due to resource lacking. What will you do?

A- Crashing
B- Fast –tracking
C- Resource leveling
D- Resource smoothing

Correct Answer
D – Resource Smoothing

Question 4

You are advising a project manager who is new to your company and has just been assigned to manage project. The sponsor on his project is very demanding and is asking to see a project schedule developed as soon as possible. The project manager would like to meet the sponsor's request and produce a project schedule as quickly as possible but without jeopardizing work quality. Which of the following represent the best advice for the project manager in this case.

A- Develop the activity list, then the WBS and the WBS dictionary
B- Develop the WBS and activity list concurrently with the help of project team members.
C- Develop the WBS and activity list concurrently using the project manager's expertise, rather than the whole project team.
D- Ask senior management for a new sponsor within the company.

Correct Answer

A – Develop the WBS and activity list concurrently with the help of project team members.

Question 5

The project is supposed to roll out a new service to thousands of existing users. The project team wants to consider and prepare for various possibilities and situations that may occur during rollout. What technique can the project manager facilitate to help learn with their preparations?

A- What- If scenario analysis
B- Critical path method
C- Fast tracking technique
D- Statistical sampling

Correct Answer

A – What- If scenario analysis

11. COST

Cost Management

Project Cost Management includes the processes involved in planning, estimating, budgeting, financing, funding, managing, and controlling costs so that the project can be completed within the approved budget. On some projects, especially those of smaller scope, cost estimating, and cost budgeting are tightly linked and can be viewed as a single process that can be performed by a single person over a relatively short period of time. These are presented here as distinct processes because the tools and techniques for each are different. The most crucial cost parameters will be managed and shared by it.

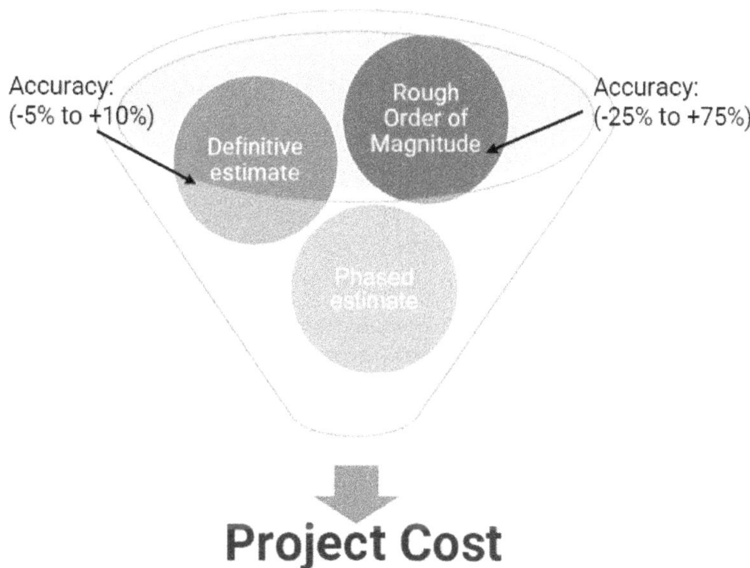

Project Cost Management is primarily concerned with the cost of the resources needed to complete project activities. Project Cost Management should also consider the effect of project decisions on the subsequent recurring cost of using, maintaining, and supporting the product, service, or result of the project.

The main goal of project cost management is to keep the project's costs under control and ensure its successful completion.

What Is Project Cost Management?

The cost management plan is a component of the project management plan and describes how the project costs will be planned, structured, and controlled. The cost management processes, and their associated tools and techniques are documented in the cost management plan.

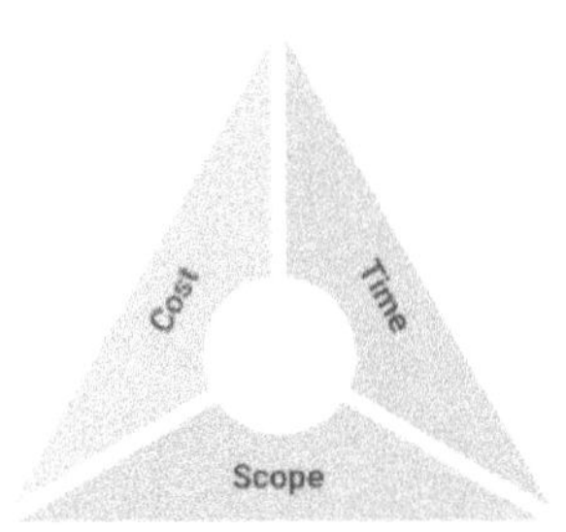

A triangle is formed by scope, schedule, and cost. Every task you want to execute for the project must be listed in the scope baseline. Next, we create the schedule baseline, which outlines the timeline for each activity and the dates on which it is going to occur.
Cost baseline is the third baseline. In the past, these three constraints—often referred to as the "iron triangle" or "triple constraints"—were thought to be the most significant.

We create a task breakdown framework for the scope baseline. Work package is the lowest level of the work breakdown hierarchy. Milestones, an activity list, and activity attributes are further broken out in the work package. From these activities, we create a critical route or network map of the project schedule. This is referred as critical path.

We then estimate the costs associated with each activity when we add the schedule baseline, which is essentially our schedule at this point. We then add the estimated costs associated with each work package, each planning package, and this control account to arrive at our cost baseline and project budget.

Scope baseline. The scope baseline includes the project scope statement and WBS detail for cost estimation and management.

Schedule baseline. The schedule baseline defines when the project costs will be incurred.

Other information. Other cost-related scheduling, risk, and communications decisions from the project management plan.

Cost Baseline

The cost baseline is the approved version of the time-phased project budget, excluding any management reserves. Can be changed only through formal change control procedures and is the basis for comparison to actual results.

- Monitors and measures cost performance.
- Includes a budget contingency.
- Is tailored for each project.

Tolerance is always within a plus-minus range. Plus, or minus 10%

Estimate Costs

Cost estimates are a prediction that is based on the information known at a given point in time. Cost estimates include the identification and consideration of costing alternatives to initiate and complete the project. Cost tradeoffs and risks should be considered, such as make versus buy, buy versus lease, and the sharing of resources in order to achieve optimal costs for the project.

Cost estimates should be reviewed and refined during the course of the project to reflect additional detail as it becomes available, and assumptions are tested.

The accuracy of a project estimate will increase as the project progresses through the project life cycle. For example, a project in the initiation phase may have a **rough order of magnitude (ROM)** estimate in the range of −25% to +75%. Later in the project, as more information is known, definitive estimates could narrow the range of accuracy to -5% to +10%.

Lessons Learned/Organizational Process Assets

How far was the budget exceeded? In the past, what procedures were used to establish the budget? How should we proceed? Once the strategy has been developed, it must be authorized. During the change management process, predictive analysis is conducted. Once a plan has been approved, only a change control board has the authority to modify it.

Estimation Techniques

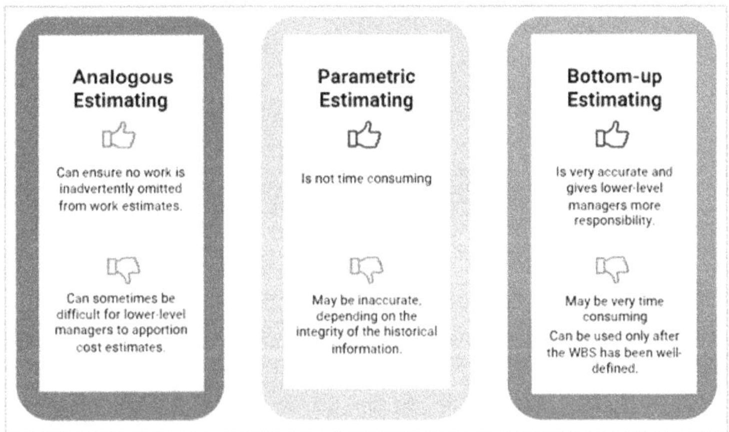

- **Analogous Estimation**

Analogous Estimation, also known as "top-down" estimation, is a technique that involves estimating the parameters of a current project by comparing them to similar past projects. This technique is particularly useful when there is limited information available about the current project, and it allows for a quick and approximate estimate of the project's parameters by using high-level information from past projects.

- **Parametric Estimation**

Parametric estimation involves using statistical relationships between historical data and other variables to calculate estimates for activity parameters. This technique can produce higher levels of accuracy depending upon the sophistication and underlying data built into the model. Parametric cost estimates can be applied to a total project or to segments of a project, in conjunction with other estimating methods.

- **Bottom-Up Estimation**

In bottom-up estimation, each work package is estimated individually, and the estimates are then aggregated to create an overall project estimate. This approach is often more accurate than top-down estimation, which involves estimating the project as a whole and then breaking it down into smaller components.

Bottom-up estimation is a time-consuming process, as it requires detailed estimates for each work package. However, it can provide a more accurate estimate of the resources required for a project, as it considers the specific requirements of each component.

Contingency Reserves

When a project is initiated, our goal is to detect as many risks as we can; if a risk is recognized, we set aside budget to tackle it; this money is referred to as contingency reserves. In case the risk materializes, we use that specific sum of money for that specific reason, allowing us to effectively mitigate the risk on the project through contingency reserves allotted for that specifically identified risks.

Activity Cost = Cost of Activity + Contingency Reserves

Work Package = Cost of that Activity (A +B +C) + Contingency Reserve

Management Reserves

The management reserve is the amount of the project budget set aside for unanticipated work that falls within the project's scope. The management reserve is added to the cost baseline, resulting in the total project budget.

When Should You Adjust the Management Reserve?

Reserves may be used, reduced, or eliminated over time. Not everyone agrees with reducing unused reserves. Project managers should determine with the project sponsor whether management reserves will be reduced or eliminated during the project, how this will occur, and when. Include this information in your Cost Management Plan.

Determine Budget

The process of aggregating the estimated costs of individual activities or work packages to establish an authorized cost baseline. The key benefit of this process is that it determines the cost baseline against which project performance can be monitored and controlled.

Project Budget

A project budget includes all the funds authorized to execute the project. The cost baseline is the approved version of the time-phased project budget but excludes management reserves.

Project Budget = Cost Baseline + Management Reserve

Now that we are aware of it, we constantly need to determine the new budget when we estimate something for a project.

Estimate at Complete (EAC)

Estimate at Complete, or EAC, is the name given to the new budget.

- Estimate at Completion= Actual Cost + Estimate to Complete
- Estimate at Completion = Budget at Completion / Cost Performance Index
- To-Complete Performance Index = Work Remaining/ Fund remaining
- If TCPI is greater than one, that means it is bad for project.

Funding Limit Reconciliation

Total funding requirements and periodic funding requirements (e.g., quarterly, annually) are derived from the cost baseline. The cost baseline will include projected expenditures plus anticipated liabilities. Funding often occurs in incremental amounts that are not continuous and may not be evenly distributed. The total funds required are those included in the cost baseline, plus management reserves, if any.

Control Costs

Control Costs is the process of monitoring the status of the project to update the project costs and managing changes to the cost baseline. The key benefit of this process is that it provides the means to recognize variance from the plan to take corrective action and minimize risk.

Project Cost Control Includes:

- Influencing the factors that create changes to the authorized cost baseline.
- Ensuring that all change requests are acted on in a timely manner.
- Managing the actual changes when and as they occur.
- Ensuring that cost expenditures do not exceed the authorized funding by period, by WBS component, by activity, and in total for the project.
- Monitoring cost performance to isolate and understand variances from the approved cost baseline.
- Monitoring work performance against funds expended.
- Preventing unapproved changes from being included in the reported cost or resource usage.
- Informing appropriate stakeholders of all approved changes and associated cost.
- Bringing expected cost overruns within acceptable limits.

Work Performance Data includes information about project progress, such as which activities have started, their progress, and which deliverables have finished. Information also includes costs that have been authorized and incurred.

Earned Value Management

A methodology that combines scope, schedule, and resource measurements to assess project performance and progress.

- **Planned Value**

The authorized budget assigned to scheduled work.

- **Earned Value**

The measure of work performed expressed in terms of the budget authorized for that work.

- **Actual Cost**

The realized cost incurred for the work performed on an activity during a specific time period.

Schedule Variance (SV) = Earned Value (EV) - Planned Value (PV)

- If schedule variance is equal to zero you are **on schedule.**
- If it is positive, you are within the budget or **ahead of schedule.**
- If it is negative, you are **behind schedule**.

Schedule Performance Index= Earned Value / Actual Cost

If SPI is,

- Equal to 1 we are **on schedule** or within the schedule.
- Less than 1 is **behind schedule.**

Cost variance = Earned Value - Actual Cost

- If cost variance is equal to zero you are **on budget**
- If it is positive, you are within the budget or **under budget.**
- If it is negative, you are spending more it is **over budget**.

Cost Performance Index = Earned Value / Actual Cost

If CPI is, Equal to 1 we are **on budget** or within the budget.

- Less than 1 is **out of budget or over budget.**

Budget at Completion (BAC)

At completion, the complete project, including the budget, is known as the BAC project.

Remaining Work = Budget at Completion – Earned Value

Remaining Funds = Budget at Completion – Actual Cost

BAC	Budget At Completion	Total Budget
PV	Planned Value	Planned % Complete x BAC
EV	Earned Value	Actual % Complete x BAC
AC	Actual Costs	Sum Of Actual Costs
CV	Cost Variance	EV - AC
SV	Schedule Variance	EV - PV
SPI	Schedule Performance Index	EV / PV
CPI	Cost Performance Index	EV / AC
EAC	Estimate At Completion	BAC / CPI
ETC	Estimate To Completion	EAC - AC
VAC	Variance At Completion	BAC - EAC
TCPI	To-Complete-Performance Index	(BAC-EV) / (BAC-AC)

PRACTICE EXAM QUESTIONS

Question 1

You are a project manager on a large scale that would involve work being performed across multiple continents. Which of the following factors are most likely to be the greatest cost risk to the project?

A. Exchange rates and Inflation
B. Poor product quality
C. Global demand fluctuations
D. Communication issues due to different language

Correct Answer

A – Exchange rates and Inflation

Question 2

A project manager was successful in his ability to obtain the three most skilled craftsmen within his company to join the project team in completion of a large industrial turbine overhaul project. The skill and experience of the craftsmen have manifested positive results. The team has been able to complete the project work faster than defined in the schedule and at a better cost efficiency rate. The project manager expects the current conditions to continue throughout the remainder of the project. Which equations should the project manager use to calculate the estimate at completion value?

A. EAC= [AC + BAC-EV/ (CPI × SPI)]
B. EAC= BAC / CPI
C. EAC= AC + (BAC-EV)
D. EAC= AC + (BAC+ EV)

Correct Answer

B – EAC= BAC/CPI

Question 3

You are running a multi-year project; Your BAC is 100,000. Your SPI is 1.2 and your CPI is 1.2. Your sponsor has asked you to reduce the schedule, which estimation technique are you going to use.

A. Crashing
B. Fast tracking
C. Resource levelling
D. Resource smoothing

Correct Answer

A – Crashing

Question 4

Analogous Estimating relies on which of the following cost technique.

A. Vendor Bid analysis.
B. Reserve Analysis
C. Project management software
D. Expert Judgment

Correct Answer

D – Expert Judgment

Question 5

Your project has a CV of 124 and SPI of 0.8 what can you tell with this information.

A. Your project is ahead of schedule and within budget.
B. Your project is over budget of schedule and ahead of schedule.
C. Your project is within the budget and behind schedule.
D. Your project is within the budget and ahead of schedule.

Correct Answer

C – Your project is within the budget and behind schedule.

12. BUSINESS ENVIRONMENT

Business Environment

In project management, the business environment refers to the external factors that can impact a project's success. These factors can include economic conditions, market trends, regulatory requirements, and technological advancements, among others.

Understanding the business environment is critical for project managers because it helps them to identify potential risks and opportunities that may impact the project. By analyzing the business environment, project managers can develop strategies to mitigate risks and take advantage of opportunities.

For example, if the business environment is highly competitive, project managers may need to focus on developing innovative solutions to differentiate their project from competitors. If the regulatory environment is complex, project managers may need to allocate additional resources to ensure compliance with regulations.

The business environment can also impact project stakeholders, including clients, suppliers, and team members. For example, changes in economic conditions may impact a client's ability to fund a project, while changes in market trends may impact the demand for a project's deliverables.

Understanding the Project Environment

There are many factors that need to be understood within your project environment.

On one level, you need to think in terms of the cultural and social environments (i.e., people, demographics, and education). The international and political environment is where you need to understand about different countries' cultural influences. Then we move to the physical environment, specifically the time zones. Think about different countries and how differently your project will be executed whether it is just in your country or if it involves an international project team that is distributed throughout the world in five different countries.

Among the various factors, the physical ones are relatively easier to understand and implement, whereas the cultural and international factors are often misinterpreted or ignored. How we interact with clients, customers, and project members from other countries can be critical to the project's success. The way a product is perceived can significantly vary based on the international cultural differences.

Project managers in multicultural projects must appreciate the culture dimensions and try to learn relevant customs, courtesies, and business protocols before taking responsibility for managing an international project. A project manager must take into consideration these various cultural influences and how they may affect the project's completion, schedule, scope, and cost.

Organizational governance framework includes elements such as rules, policies and procedures, systems, relationships, and norms. Developing the Project Management Plan help to frame the culture and behavior of the organization, which will in turn influence the project, the risk tolerance of the organization, and how people perform.

It is important to note that management elements are influenced according to the organizational structure (i.e., functional, matrix, or project-oriented) and the organizational governance framework. Example management elements include how work is distributed, authority levels of workers, disciplinary actions, chain of command, fair treatment of employees, fair payment for work performed, communication channels, safety of staff members, morale, and more.

Project Governance consists of framework, functions, and processes that guide project management activities to create a unique product, service, or result to meet organizational, strategic, and operational goals. With a strong, robust project governance model in place, the overall framework of the project can maximize the project's success.

Project Governance Framework – Components

- Project success and deliverable acceptance criteria.
- The process to identify, escalate and resolve issues.
- Relationship between the project team, organizational groups, and external stakeholders.
- Project organization chart with project roles.
- Communication processes and procedures.
- Processes for decision-making.
- Guidelines for aligning project governance and organizational strategy.
- Project lifecycle approach.
- Process for Stage-Gate of phase views.
- Process for review and approval of changes above the project managers' authority.
- The process to align internal stakeholders to project process requirements.

Consequently, the organizational chart contains numerous laws and regulations. Who are the decision-making authorities, and how do they oversee all aspects of project governance? A governance committee oversees and governs the entire board, as well overseeing all your operations and ensuring the project is completed as efficiently as possible.

PHASE-TO-PHASE RELATIONSHIPS:

1- **Sequential relationships** contain consecutive phases that start only when the previous phase is complete. This relationship reduces the level of uncertainty, which may eliminate the option of shortening a project schedule.
2- **Overlapping relationships** contain phases that start before the previous phase ends. This relationship increases the level of risk and may cause rework. If something from the previous phase directly affects the next phase.

<u>Phase Gate</u> is a review at the end of a phase in which a decision is made to continue to the next phase, to continue with modification, or to end a project or program.

Determine appropriate Governance for a Project:

- Involves the organization's decision managers i.e., senior managers.
- Choose the most appropriate governance goals and try to keep them simple.
- Select a group of experienced individuals to be responsible for all governance activities.

Compliance:

Compliance refers to the act of conforming to a set of standards, rules, laws, or requirements that are relevant to the project. Compliance ensures that projects are executed in accordance with organizational policies, industry regulations, and legal requirements. It plays a crucial role in minimizing risks, maintaining transparency, and ensuring good governance throughout the project's lifecycle.

Projects must be compliant with internal and external standards. Compliance with:

- Appropriate government regulations
- Corporate policies
- Product, project quality
- Project risk

A project compliance plan is a sub-plan of the project management plan which includes:

- Classifying compliance categories.
- Determining potential threats to compliance.
- Analyzing the consequences of non-compliance.
- Determining the necessary approach, and action to address compliance needs.

Noncompliance with project requirements poses a significant threat and should be avoided at all costs. Failure to comply is viewed as a negative outcome, and it is crucial to identify and manage compliance risks. Project managers must strive to reduce and address compliance issues by exploring potential solutions to mitigate their impact.

- Compliance can occur both within and outside of the organization.
- Compliance can occur anywhere in the world.

As a result, it is essential to establish specific criteria, known as compliance requirements, to meet statutory obligations. These requirements must be identified and adhered to, including those related to health, safety, and privacy regulations.

To ensure compliance, we categorize these items as follows:

Potential Threats to Compliance.

- **Identification** of new vulnerabilities.
- **Changes** in legal or regulatory requirements.
- **Errors** in testing and validation to confirm compliance.
- **Errors** or **bugs** in deliverables.
- **Lack of awareness** of compliance requirements.

TIP: If you do not know about compliance damage – use the risk register to detect the compliance, record it in the register, and deal with it appropriately.

Compliance-Related Risk, track and manage compliance-related risk on the risk register.

For compliance-related risks include:

- The identified risk
- Risk owner
- Impact of the realized risk
- Risk Responses
- Creating testing and validation plans to ensure project deliverables meet compliance.

Staying relevant in today's business environment is a fundamental challenge for all organizations. Relevance entails being responsive to stakeholder needs and desires. This requires continually evaluating offerings for the benefit of stakeholders, rapidly responding to changes, and acting as agents for change. Project managers are uniquely poised to keep an organization prepared for changes. Projects, by their very definition, create something new: they are agents of change.

Therefore, we need to ensure that whatever the project's needs were, the project met those compliance standards, and we got the desired result. We constantly report to the team and review our risk register when we deal with others to ensure compliance, and we continuously perform variance analysis to see where we should go to make the necessary changes.

Variance Analysis create regular reports on Project variances and details of actions taken to control and keep the project on track. Variances related to compliance are critical because of the potential impact on the usability of the deliverable. Variance analysis should include:

- **The identification** of the variant.
- **Plans** for bringing the project or deliverable back into compliance.
- Any proposed **changes** are required to meet compliance requirements.

Compliance signoffs and approvals identify stakeholders authorized to sign off and approve compliance of deliverables. Benefits of compliance sign off early warning of potential threats to compliance.

The ability to capture variances and determine a course of action. This step follows successful testing and validating of deliverables, but this can be done throughout the project or at the completion.

Remediate Compliance issues to avoid:

- Negative impact on the timeline
- Cost overruns
- Increased risks.

Guidelines to analyze the Consequences of Compliance:
To identify and manage legal, regulatory, and other compliance requirements:

Define:

- Legal, regulatory, and another constraint.
- The business rules constrain the project solution and improve the likelihood of compliance.
- Part of the potential solutions is subject to compliance requirements.
- The scope of the compliance requirement.
- The stakeholders are responsible for reviewing, approving, and signing off on compliance.
- **Track and manage** the review and approval activities related to **compliance** requirement.
- The risk and risk response are related to compliance requirements.

Measure Process Compliance

- Establishes a clear Quality Management Plan and act on it continuously to identify nine non-compliance issues as early as possible.
- Use quality outputs to confirm deliverable and process compliance and identify needs for corrective actions.

- Establish project tolerances and either initiate corrective actions yourself or quickly escalate non-compliance beyond the tolerances.
- Establish where the external audit team confirms and validate the use of appropriate process and procedures and how audit results can enable the team to identify improvements.
- Leverage effective quality tools and techniques to assess quality deliverables and identify improvements, corrective actions, or defect repairs requirements required.

Net Promoter Score (NPS)

NPS is a metric used in customer experience programs to measure customer satisfaction and loyalty based on the following question:

"What level of satisfaction do you have with the services?" Similar to a litmus test, NPS assesses customer satisfaction on a scale of one to ten. (10 being highly satisfied, 6 being neutral, and 1 being highly dissatisfied)

While scrolling through your screens, you might have come across a personalized ad on YouTube or Facebook. Used in marketing, **A/B testing is a method for determining user preferences to optimize the solutions offered.** They show you one or two advertisements. When you click on it or any icon, you will notice that you are viewing the same videos repeatedly. This is referred to as A/B testing (Alpha- Beta Testing).

Kaizen is seen as a model of constant progress. Kaizen is a Japanese phrase that translates to "constant improvement without cost." The name of the game is continuous progress. You can be great for a day, but continuing progress takes time and work. So, how can we work daily, and how can we enhance it?

Six Sigma

- Responds to the customer needs and improves processes by systematically removing.
- Break quality management into quality planning, control, and improvement.
- Continuous process improvement in which quality must be continuously improved to meet customer needs.
- Four absolutes: conforming to requirements, the quality achieved by prevention standard of zero defects, and quality measured determining CoQ.
- Design quality in products or factors that cause variation can be identified and controlled.

Various theories establish various practices, the idea is that you plan what you do, study it, and then act on it. Some individuals say **Plan Do Check Act**, while others say **Plan Do study Act** - both expressions mean the same thing. As a result, we implement Kaizen (minor improvements) regularly.

Continuous Improvement Approaches: Plan, Do, Study, Act

Have you wondered how can we work on something while trying to enhance it? We are aware of the need of identifying the problem, determine the solution, and implement the solution. In this case, we employ whatever is effective to solve the situation. We are already familiar with how to conduct the lesson learned, so with PDSA we will learn how to conduct this retrospective and various types of experiments to keep improving.

Plan - Define objectives and processes being tested.
Do - Run the test, describe what happens and collect data.
Study - Evaluate data and compare results to expectations.
Act - Identify issues and root causes, then modify to improve the process.

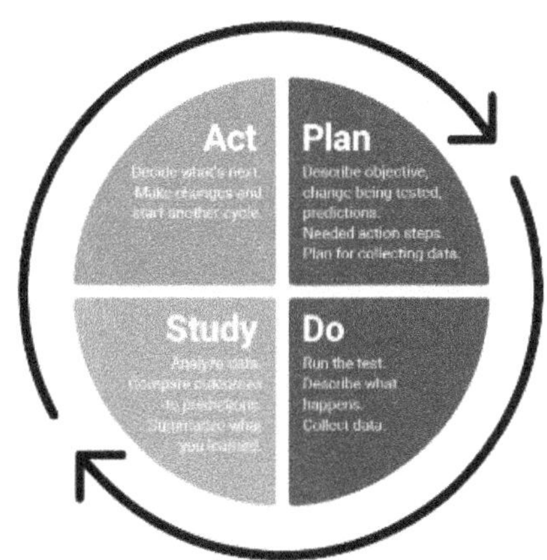

PRACTICE EXAM QUESTIONS

Question 1

Last year your company released a new service based on project you managed. The company wants to determine if the new service has increased customer satisfaction. Which tool can measure the happiness of users of the new service based on their willingness to encourage others to use your service against those who would discourage others to use your service?

A- AB Testing

B- ROI

C- NPS Score

D- Payback Period

Correct Answer

C – NPS Score

Question 2

Due to regulatory changes, a government agency is now a key stakeholder on a complex project. The project manager wants to develop an understanding of this new project stakeholder and any new high-level risks. What should the project manager use?

A- Benefit Management Plan

B- Stakeholder Engagement Plan

C- Assumption Log

D- Meeting

Correct answer

D – Meeting

Question 3

The methodology used to systematically test possible solutions, assess the results, and implement those that work is known as which of the following.

A- Retrospective
B- Continuous Improvement
C- Kaizen
D- Plan do study act.

Correct answer
D – Plan do study act

Question 4
The project team learns there is a new compliance requirement from an international entity that may impact the approved business case for the project. They learn this right after the project charter is completed and the project sponsor has signed. How the project manager should proceed.

A- Address the requirement through the creation of a quality management plan.
B- Research the requirement and possible consequences, then give the sponsor a recommendation.
C- Decline to address the issue, as the new requirement is not part of the project documented scope.
D- Ensure that the requirement is documented in the risk register, then ask for further guidance from all stakeholders.

Correct answer
B – Research the requirement and possible consequences, then give the sponsor a recommendation.

Question 5
As a result of multiple regulatory changes, a governmental agency is added as a key stakeholder on a complex project, the project manager wants to develop an understanding to this new stakeholder and identify any new high-level risks that may result from the change.

A- Meet with new stakeholders.
B- Check with the sponsor regarding the benefits management plan.
C- Identify needed changes to the assumption log.
D- Review stakeholder engagement plan

Correct answer

A – Meet with new stakeholders.

13. INTEGRATION

Project Integration Management

Integration refers to the process of coordinating all aspects of a project to ensure that it is completed successfully. Integration involves bringing together all the different components of a project, including scope, schedule, budget, resources, and stakeholders, and ensuring that they work together seamlessly.

The integration process begins during the planning phase of a project and continues throughout the project's lifecycle. It involves identifying and managing project dependencies, risks, and issues, as well as ensuring that all project components are aligned with the project's goals and objectives.

The need for Project Integration Management is necessary in situations where individual processes interact. For example, a cost estimate needed for a contingency plan involves integrating the processes in the Project Cost, Time, and Risk Management Knowledge Areas. When additional risks associated with various staffing alternatives are identified, then one or more of those processes may be revisited. The project deliverables may also need integrating with ongoing operations of the performing organization, the requesting organization, and with the long-term strategic planning that takes future problems and opportunities into consideration. Project Integration Management also includes the activities needed to manage project documents to ensure consistency with the project management plan and product, service, or capability deliverables.

The project manager is responsible for integrating all project plans. The primary responsibility of the project manager is to develop and obtain approval for project management plans. These plans include a strategy, as well as a configuration management plan and a change management plan. The change management plan is designed to monitor any changes to the project, while the configuration management plan is updated to reflect any changes made. The term "by-product" refers to the entire process from project conception to completion. Therefore, change management is examined both within and outside the project domain to ensure effective management of changes.

Integration management:

- Assessment and coordination of all plans and activities that are built, maintained, and executed throughout a project.
- A holistic, integrated view ties plans together aligns efforts, and highlights how they depend on each other.
- An integrated view of all plans can identify and correct gaps or conflicts.
- A consolidation of the plans encapsulates the overall project plan and its intended business value.

Develop Project Management Plan

Develop Project Management Plan is the process of defining, preparing, and coordinating all subsidiary plans and integrating them into a comprehensive project management plan. The key benefit of this process is a central document that defines the basis of all project work.

Steps of the Project Management Plan:

- Make
- Execute
- Manage
- Handle
- Close

Project managers use a variety of tools and techniques to manage project integration, including project management software, stakeholder engagement strategies, and change management processes. By effectively managing project integration, project managers can ensure that their projects are completed successfully and deliver the desired outcomes.

Project management is all about managing change, and how you handle changes in the project. Alternatively, configuration management is concerned with dealing with product modifications.

Configuration Management Plan

- Identify and account out for project artifacts under configuration control, how to record and report changes to them.
- Identification, maintenance, status, reporting, and verification of configuration items.

Change Management Plan

A component of the project management plan that establishes the change control board, documents the extent of its authority, and describes how the change control system will be implemented. Change Management Plan will evaluate the following questions:

- Who can propose a change?
- What exactly constitutes a change?
- What is the impact of the change in the project's objectives?
- What steps are necessary to evaluate the change request before approving or rejecting it?
- When a change request is approved, what project documents must be amended to record the actions necessary to effort to the change?
- How will these actions be monitored to confirm that they have been completed satisfactorily?

Project documents are integral documents for a project; they are regularly updated by project management processes.

Deliverables any unique and verifiable product, result, or capability (tangible or intangible) to perform a service that is required to be produced to complete a process, phase, or project.

- Key outputs are referring to the item identified in the scope statement and WBS.
- Change Control should be applied once the first version of the deliverable has been completed.
- Control of multiple versions of a deliverable, for example, document, software, and box are done according to configuration management tools and procedures.

Storage And Distribution of Artifacts

- Store artifacts in an accessible location for users.
- Use a storage distribution system that matches the complexity of the project.
- Use cloud-based document storage and retrieval systems for larger projects, especially where team members are geographically distributed.
- Typical systems may include:
- Built-in version control
- Document check out and check-in.
- User-based documents security
- Automatic email notification to specified users when a document is created or edited.

Causes of Project Changes

- Inaccurate initial estimates.
- Specification changes,
- New regulation.
- Missed requirement.

Preventive action, corrective action, and defect correction are all options. If you do not take preventive action, chances are something unfortunate could happen. We examine the plan, act, and enhance it to prevent the problem from occurring. However, we may still change it by taking remedial action. If something terrible has happened and there is nothing, we can do about it, we need to alter our defect-repair strategy. Then there are updates along the road of course. As a result, we make those modifications to boost the business value.

Change Control System

A set of procedures that describes how modifications to the project deliverables and documentation are managed and controlled. It establishes the following questions:

- How do we track the changes?
- What are the processes that are involved?
- How do we approve those changes?

Change Control Board (CCB):

A formally chartered group responsible for reviewing, evaluating, approving, delaying, or rejecting changes to the project and for recording and communicating such decisions.

Change Management Process Flowchart:

The purpose of the change management process is to manage change requests so that approved changes will be controlled, ensuring the project remains on schedule, within budget and provides the agreed deliverables.

Step 1: Identify and Submit a Change Request
This process provides the ability to submit a request for a change to the project. The Change Requester:

- Identifies a requirement for change to any aspect of the project (e.g., scope, deliverables, schedule, and organization)
- Completes a Change Request Form (CRF) and submits the form to the Project Manager.

Step 2: Review the Change Request
The Project Manager and Lead reviews the Change Request and determines whether additional information is required for CCB to assess the full impact of the change to the project time, scope, and cost. The decision will be based on factors, such as:

- Number of change options presented.
- Feasibility and benefits of the change
- Complexity and/or difficulty of the change options requested.
- Scale of the change solutions proposed.

Step 3: Approval of the Change Request
The Project Manager will forward the Change Request Form and any supporting documentation to Change Control Board for review and final approval. The CCB will determine the feasibility of this change by examining factors, such as:

- Risk to the project in implementing the change.
- Risk to the project in NOT implementing the change.
- Impact on the project in implementing the change (time, resources, cost, quality).

Step 4: After a formal review, the Change Control Board may:

- Reject the change.
- Request more information related to the change.
- Approve the change as requested.
- Approve the change subject to specified conditions.
- Escalate the change.

Step 5: Closing the Change Request
If the change is approved, the following will occur:

- The change will be communicated to the team.
- Project deliverables will be updated to reflect the change.
- The change request will be closed.
- All approved change requests will be communicated in the Project status report.

Issues are a current condition or situation that may have on the project objectives-an action item that the project team must address. Issue can affect,

- Quality
- Scope
- Schedule

How to Handle Issues?

- As issues arise promptly add them to the issue log.
- Assign an owner to each issue.
- The owner is responsible for tracking the progress of the workaround and reporting back.
- Give realistic due dates and make every reasonable attempt to meet them.
- Issues should be a regular topic of every status meeting.
- Limit the number of open issues to a manageable number.

- Do not hesitate to escalate an issue to the project sponsor if it begins to have a major effect on the project.

Resolving issues:

- Use your organization's issue log template in the absence of one to create an issue log.
- Train project team members to promptly report potential issues.
- Enter the issue into the issue log and assign an owner and due date.
- Monitor progress and discuss each open issue at every project status meeting.
- Developer response is also known as a workaround, to the issues.
- Assess the impact of the response.
- Approve the response.
- Close the issue.

Knowledge Management is the process of identifying, organizing, storing, and disseminating information within an organization.

Explicit knowledge

- Can be codified by using symbols such as words, numbers, and pictures.
- Can be documented and shared with others.

Tacit knowledge

- Personal knowledge that can be difficult to articulate and share such as beliefs, experience, and insights.
- Essential to providing the context of the explicit knowledge.

Knowledge Transfer Techniques:

- Networking & facilitating special interest groups.
- Meetings, seminars, and various other types of in-person and virtual events encourage people to interact and exchange ideas and knowledge.
- Training that involves interaction between attendees
- Work shadowing and reverse shadowing provide a more individualized method to exchange specialized knowledge.

Considerations for Lessons Learned:

Schedule at the **right time**, include topics on:

- Conflict Management
- Vendor Relationships
- Customers
- Strategy
- Tactics

Lessons Learned Register: A project document used to record knowledge gained during a project so that it can be used in the current project and entered the lessons-learned repository.

Lessons-Learned Repository: A store of historical information about lessons learned in projects.

Close Project or Phase Criteria:

Closure Reasons:

- The project or phase successfully made its completion objectives.
- Requirement change during execution and the project is no longer feasible.
- Funding is no longer available to complete the requirements.

- Significant risk makes the successful completion of the project impossible.
- The organization no longer needs the project and deliverables.
- External factors eliminate the need for the project.

Examples of these factors include:

- Changes in laws or regulations
- Merger or acquisition that affects the organization.
- Global or national economic changes

Payments:

- Payments made to a supplier or vendor are made by the terms of contract between the buyer and the seller or vendor.
- Unless a contract is closed after the project or phase payment will most likely have been made at the time of contract closure.
- It should not be delayed until project or phase closure (unless specified in a contract) to avoid the potential for accidental changes in the contract.

VII) QUICK RECAP

FOR THIS [KEYWORDS]	DO THIS [RECOMMENDATION]
Project Charter	Refer for High Level Information
Business Case	Refer for Cost-Benefit Analysis
Benefit Management Plan	Intangible Value
Compliance Requirement	Found in Risk Register
Unidentified Event Happened/Occurred	Update Issue Log
Manage Quality/ Efficiency required	Audit
Control Quality/QC	Inspection, Reactive, Detecting Defects, Ensure Expected Results
Quality Assurance/QA	Proactive, preventing defects, Ensure right thing in a right way
Reviews	Inspection
Pareto Chart	20/80 Principle, Vital few, Trivial many
Design of X (DoX)	Optimizes the design.
Progressive elaboration Or Rolling Wave Planning	Both used in Predictive Lifecycle, in planning phase.

Co-relation	Scatter Diagram
Verified Deliverables	By Team
Validate Deliverables	By Customer/Client
Project Constraints	Guidelines and Policies
Tracing Requirements to the Project Scope and WBS deliverables	Requirement Traceability Matrix (RTM)
Definition of Ready	Checklist shows the requirements needed to complete tasks.
Definition of Done	Checklist of criteria that must be completed for a project/sprint to be considered "done"
Acceptance Criteria	Checklist provided by customer (Scope defined by customer, in AGILE)
Team Charter	Decision making, set ground rules.
Scrum Master	Encourage Team to self-assign the tasks.
Project Manager in Agile	Proactively manage the conflicts
New Project Manager	Must Review the Issue Log to ensure issues are

	captured, Validate the Project Artifacts/document, and do Earned Value Analysis to measure a Project Progress
To gain a consensus	Conduct a Retrospective
Forcing Power	Decides in favor of one party.
Unclear tasks assignment and Ownership	Refer to the RACI Chart
Key word INFORM/Information	PM should refer to COMMUNICATION MANAGEMENT PLAN
Important thing before Meeting	Set the Meeting Agenda
TCPI less than 1	Within budget and have done excellent job managing project cost/ BEST
TCPI greater than 1	Exceed the project budget / BAD.
TCPI=1	Right on BUDGET/ GOOD
An additional cost has incurred.	Perform integrated Change Control
Staffing Occurs	At Execution Level

If Team wants to Improve their Skills	Review the Resource Management Plan
If an unidentified risk has occurred	Update the issue log
Project Management Methodology	System of practices, techniques, procedures, and rules used by those who work in a discipline.
Cycle Time	Start-to-finish time required to develop a potentially shippable product increment.
Lead Time	Lead time is the measurement of how much time passes between task creation and when the work is completed.
Burn-up chart	How much activities have been done/completed.
Burn-down chart.	Activities not yet completed + Remaining Time in Agile
Benefits Realization Plan	A document outlining the activities necessary for achieving the planned benefits.
When extensive knowledge of the best practices in the industry required	Benchmarking is a key part of effective project management as it allows

	the project manager to compare with other players in the market.
To predict your project future performance based on the actual performance to date.	Time series, scenario building, and simulation along with regression analysis, expert opinion, and causal/econometric methods.
Contract most suitable for Agile Projects?	Time & Material
Anything Related to Procurement	Review the contract to find the next step.
To reduce Quality inspection	Do Statistical Sampling
If an identified risk has occurred	Update the risk register
Technique to minimize the scope creep.	Time boxing in Agile
Risk is Identified	Throughout the Project
Resource Management Plan	Includes Training, Team Development, Roles and Responsibility, Project Organization Chart, Recognition Plan
An appropriate way of Handling Team Conflicts?	Team ground rules, group norms, and solid project management practices, like communication

	planning and role definition, reduce the amount of conflict.
Procurement Statement of Work (SOW)	Includes specification, desired quality, performance data, period of performance, work location and other requirements.
Seller Performance Evaluation	Rates how well the seller is performing the work or has performed in the past.
Nodding the heads	Active Listening required means acknowledgment required, confirming, clarifying, understanding, and removing comm. barriers.

VIII) How To Solve PMP Exam Questions?

STEP 1: Read the Question Carefully.

- This is a very important step, most of the time we try to read questions at a fast pace, and as a result we have to re-read questions again and again . Please note you have 230 Minutes in PMP exam. Time management is the key. It is recommended to divide your time as follows;

  80 Minutes to the first 60 question, then 10-minute break, 75 minutes for the next 60 questions, another 10-minute break, and the last 75 minutes to the last 60 Questions.

- Time management can only be maintained if you slow down your brain to find and try to understand the context of the question. When you slow down, your brain will start looking for reasons to slow down and you will be able to Focus.

STEP 2: Read the Last Line First.

This is most effective when you have a question with more than 3 lines; most of the time question is actually in the last line. This can help you save time when you are running out of time. For example,

[What would the Project Manager]
- Do next?
- Should have done?
- How can this be avoided?

- [An Issue has occurred]
- Best way to resolve?
- Which plan to update?
- Which document to update?

This helps you to master the question in a better way.

STEP 3: Identify the Keywords.

If you can identify the keywords correctly, the question is yours. Some keywords are like,

- Risk has occurred, Issue has occurred.
- An unidentified event has occurred
- A stakeholder is added, and a new stakeholder is identified
- You want to communicate
- The project is closed/ canceled
- Deliverable is rejected.
- You are reviewing the project
- Change has been raised/ Approved

STEP 4: Identify Context/Process Group Mentioned in Question.

Knowing the context of the question and mastering where you are in a particular process group can help you to solve questions in a better way. These are some tips to know where you are.

- Initiation – Only the project charter, assumption log, and stakeholder register are made.

- Planning – All the plans are made in this process and most of the document, this step is all about HOW to do something not done.

- Execution- Work is being done in this process group, issues are generated, the team comes here, conflicts happen, and communication occurs. Everything is done in the process. If the question indicate happening you are here.

- Monitoring and control – Variance analysis, you are comparing the plan to the actual and raising change request, deliverables are verified and accepted here.

- Closing – Project is ending, document and Lesson learned, Final report team realize

STEP 5: Identify and Select Life Cycle.

In 2022, PMP exam has been dominated by agile process group. However, according to PMP Exam content outline, It should be 50% predictive and 50% hybrid. This mean it can change any day. It is important to know the differences and use of all life cycle.

- Predictive- Scope is fixed, and Delivery is single. Risk is less, project are known and less uncertain, to raise change request needs approval, make plan for everything example – a construction project.

- Iterative – Single delivery; however, scope can be added or removed at any time Example - Prototype.

- Incremental – Delivery in part, the scope is fixed, for example, E-learning, Series.

- Agile – Delivery can be part, scope is adjustable, the customer is king, the team is self-organized.

- Hybrid – Can be a combination of any two (Predictive & Agile)

- Please note in #PMP exam if you cannot find the word agile or predictive written, assume it's a hybrid question.

STEP 6: Understand the Role in Context.

After you've identified the keyword, derived the lifecycle in question and realized the context of question, DETERMINE whose responsibility would it to be perform the duty asked.

For example, following are 4 critical roles associated with performing high level **project management duties in PREDICTIVE ENVIRONMENT.**

- Project Sponsor – Determines the budget, approves the project charter and signs off the project.
- Project Manager – Determines the methodology used, resolves conflicts, negotiates with various project stakeholders and facilitates and integrates the overall project work
- Change Control Board – Committee responsible for formally approving or rejecting the change requested.
- Project Team - Contributes to overall project objectives, provides expertise, and documents the process.

We have the following ROLES in AGILE METHODOLOGY.

- Scrum Master/ Servant leader - Works to fulfill the needs of the teams, projects, and organization. Servant leaders facilitate, coach, and removes impediments for the development team.
- Product Owner: Also known as the voice of customer, works with stakeholders, customers, and the teams to define the product direction. Responsible for creating the product backlog.
- Cross Functional Team: Team members with all the skills necessary to produce a working product.

STEP 7: Use Elimination Technique to Solve PMP Question.

- If you don't do what I have shared in the first 5 Steps, follow this step religiously. You will get 80% of question right (Provided that you master the PMP material)
- What is the Elimination technique? You must have a justification of each and every step of the question.
- Let's say you go to option A and you feel option A is the right answer, you must justify it in your mind with WHY? This is the right answer, but don't select it. Mark it, go to the next option. Now option B seems as wrong option, you must justify why you think it is the wrong Option. Now option C again seems as right option you must justify why it seems as a right option and mark it. Now option D may seem wrong again. Justify why it's wrong.
- In a normal PMP scenario, you are left with two best options (Please note, it is possible you may have selected option A and moved forward. This is against the principle of Elimination techniques. You must go to each and every option. Never rush)
- Now two options use same technique justify which option makes more sense, go for it.

STEP 8: Identify Root Cause / Lesson Learned After Solving Questions.

- Now that you have solved the question, should you move to next mock? NO!
- Otherwise, you will make the same mistakes again and again. Please stop here!
- Identify what you did wrong and why you did it wrong. What did you learn from this particular question?

- Use an excel file as a lesson learned template and review your lesson learned to find out which topics you are getting the most question wrong and improve it. Keep doing it and you will become PMP.

- Please note that this is considered as most important step by our certified professionals.

IX) Common mistakes to avoid when taking the PMP exam:

- Not studying enough: The PMP exam is a challenging exam that requires a significant amount of preparation. Not following a roadmap or studying enough can lead to poor performance on the exam.

- Not understanding the exam format: The PMP exam is a computer-based exam that consists of 180 multiple-choice questions. It is important to understand the exam format and how to navigate through the questions.

- Not reading the questions carefully: The PMP exam questions can be complex and require careful reading to fully understand what is being asked. Rushing through the questions can lead to misinterpretation and incorrect answers.

- Not managing time effectively: The PMP exam is timed, and it is important to manage time effectively to ensure that all questions are answered within the allotted time.

- Not practicing with sample questions: Practicing with sample questions can help you become familiar with the exam format and types of questions that will be asked. Not practicing with sample questions can lead to poor performance on the exam.

- Overthinking options: Sometimes, the answer to a question is straightforward, and overthinking it can lead to confusion and incorrect answers. Use elimination technique.

- Not answering all questions: It is important to answer all questions, even if you are not sure of the answer. Leaving questions unanswered can result in lost points.

- Not taking breaks: The PMP exam is a long exam that can be mentally exhausting. Taking breaks can help you stay focused and refreshed throughout the exam.

By avoiding these common mistakes, you can increase your chances of passing the PMP exam and earning your certification. It is important to prepare thoroughly and approach the exam with a clear and focused mindset.

X) Points to remember for the PMP Exam

PREDICTIVE

- Identification and analysis of stakeholders is something that is done throughout the project not just at the beginning.

- Always follow a plan and never allow changes to the plan without an approved change request.

- Any stakeholder that wants to change any component of the project management plan will need to submit a change request.

- All change requests will need to be reviewed and assessed.

- Never take actions without first creating a plan.

- Consult with the project team before making decisions, as they will have a more practical approach.

- Your final decision should always benefit the objectives of the project. For example, if there are conflicting methods on how to complete a particular task, then choose the method that would deliver the most value to the project outcome.

- Try to use tools that are inclusive such as a whiteboard with a marker versus complex software.

- All scope changes should be assessed on how it will impact all other parts of the project including schedule, cost, quality, resources, communications, risk, procurement, and stakeholders' engagement.

- When conducting estimating uses a bottom-up approach and not a top-down. This will lead to more correct estimates but will require more work.

- Your main job is to be an integrator of the many different components within a project. Do not concentrate your time and efforts on one particular thing while ignoring others.

- Update the lesson learned register throughout the entire project. This way it can be transferred to future projects in the organization.

- When closing the project ensure all bills are paid off and resources are released.

- Projects that are terminated early still needs to be close formally through the close project or phase process.

- The best people to determine when a particular activity may happen is the project team.

- Quality requirements should be defined early in the project and be checked often to ensure they are getting done.

- The customers are the best people to check a deliverable for scope conference and quality requirements being met as they are the ones that will actually use the product.

- Before resolving a conflict between team members be sure to understand the source of the conflict.

- Conflicts between team members should always be resolved for the benefits of the project objectives.

- Before communications are sent out to stakeholders, ensure to analyze their needs, and determine what they are looking for, how often, what method they would like it to be delivered, and who will deliver it to them.

- Utilize the skills of emotional intelligence to analyze your own feelings and those around you to respond to stakeholders' needs and requirements. Emotional intelligence allows you to solve problems quicker and more effectively.

- Identify as much risk as possible as early as possible on a project. All identified risks should be documented in the risk register along with their corresponding risk responses.

- A negative risk is known as a threat while positive risk is known as an opportunity. Ensure to identify and document responses to both.

- When selecting a contract to use on a project with potential sellers, always use a contract that is mutually beneficial to both the seller and the buyer to the overall benefits of the project objectives.

- Engage stakeholder often and regularly. Use things such as meetings, one-on-one conversations, phone calls, and presentations to engage them.

- When engaging your stakeholders ensure they understand the communications that they are receiving. Tailor your communication to individual stakeholder needs.

AGILE

- Be a servant leader to the team at all times. This includes empowering them and removing any impediments. Give them the tools they need to succeed while staying out of their way.

- Engage the product owner to document the features and to prioritize them in the product backlog.

- Only the product owner can prioritize the features in the product backlog. If the product owner refuses to do so because they feel all of them are valuable, then you must train them on the benefits of doing so. DO NOT prioritize the features yourself, this is the job of the product owner.

- Face-to-face communications with a white board and markers are the best form of communications.

- Provide agile teams with lots of wall space so they can write on them and use sticky notes.

- Information should always be radiated using large charts and graphs, such as the use of a burnup or burned down chart.
- Any problem that occurs on a project should be resolved by the project team. Always let the project team choose a solution while coaching and supporting their solutions.

- Provide a safe environment for disagreements. Do not punish anyone for having a difference of opinion.

- Understand that conflicts are a positive step and opportunity to learn.

- Try to limit the work in progress using the Kanban. Kanban boards should be displayed either on a large whiteboard or less desirable large monitor.

- Consistently communicate and re-communicate the project vision to the team.

- Understand the needs of your team members and find out what may motivate them.

- Make sure people understand what failure and success will look like on the project.

- Have good ethical values and be a central figure to the team, not a dictator.

- Review the methods work was completed by doing a retrospective.

- Utilize feedback loops. Feedback loops occurs when you have completed the task and then take what you have learned from that and input the lessons learned into your next task.

XI) References:

A Guide to the Project Management Body of Knowledge – (PMBOK® Guide) – Seventh Edition

A Guide to the Project Management Body of Knowledge – (PMBOK® Guide) – Fifth Edition

https://www.edureka.co/blog/project-management/https://www.researchgate.net/figure/The-Triple-Constraints-5_fig6_297922488

https://blogs.sap.com/2020/12/21/why-agile-or-why-not/

https://www.researchgate.net/figure/Method-of-interest-importance-influence-power-matrix-31_fig3_348258645

https://www.sketchbubble.com/en/presentation-elements-of-communication.html

https://www.nulivo.com/items/402/tuckman-s-team-development-model-google-slides-diagrams

https://www.researchgate.net/figure/Maslows-Need-Hierarchy-Maslow-1943_fig1_329528332
https://www.qualitygurus.com/conflict-resolution-thomas-kilmann-model/

https://www.nvisia.com/insights/agile-methodology

http://interview-questions-project-manager.blogspot.com/2015/06/the-5-scopes-of-agile-planning.html

https://storiesonboard.com/blog/moscow-prioritization-model

https://www.researchgate.net/figure/The-red-curve-is-the-cumulative-distribution-function-CDF-based-on-the-mean-and_fig3_327320528

https://ftmaintenance.com/wp-content/uploads/2020/02/Root-Cause-Analysis-Fishbone-Diagram-768x379.jpg

https://wikieducator.org/Educational_Statistics

https://corporatefinanceinstitute.com/resources/management/make-or-buy-decision/

https://project-management.com/requirements-traceability-matrix-rtm/#what-elements-should-an-rtm-include

https://powerslides.com/powerpoint-business/project-management-templates/project-scope-template/

https://www.slideteam.net/five-phases-for-project-management-funnel.html

https://blog.ganttpro.com/en/how-to-create-a-work-breakdown-structure-wbs-with-project-planning-templates/

https://powerslides.com/powerpoint-business/project-management-templates/project-scope-template/

https://www.apm.org.uk/resources/find-a-resource/gantt-chart/

https://www.projectcubicle.com/project-scheduling-steps/

https://t2informatik.de/en/smartpedia/work-breakdown-structure/

https://monday.com/blog/project-management/how-network-diagrams-help-project-management-teams-visualize-their-workflows/

https://bordio.com/blog/project-management-triangle/

https://slidebazaar.com/items/pestle-analysis-powerpoint-template/https://medpeds.ucla.edu/advocate/anti-vaping-champions/clinical-support/avc-clinical-qi-process

www.ingramcontent.com/pod-product-compliance
Lightning Source LLC
LaVergne TN
LVHW021136160826
845679LV00023B/1930

9798891867062